RIGHT TURN

RIGHT TURN
How the Tories Took Ontario

CHRISTINA BLIZZARD

DUNDURN PRESS
Toronto • Oxford

Cover photograph by Frank Iusi; artistic director: Lynne Atkinson
Cover concept by Ian Payton
Edited by Michael Power
Printed and bound in Canada by Webcom

The publisher wishes to acknowledge the generous assistance and ongoing support of the **Canada Council**, the **Book Publishing Industry Development Program** of the **Department of Canadian Heritage**, the **Ontario Arts Council**, the **Ontario Publishing Centre** of the **Ministry of Citizenship, Culture and Recreation**, and the **Ontario Heritage Foundation**.
    Care has been taken to trace the ownership of copyright material used in the text (including the illustrations). The author and publisher welcome any information enabling them to rectify any reference or credit in subsequent editions.

J. Kirk Howard, Publisher

Canadian Cataloguing in Publication Data

Blizzard, Christina, 1948–
    Right turn : how the Tories took Ontario

Includes index
ISBN 1-55002-254-7

1. Ontario. Legislative Assembly – Elections, 1995.
2. Ontario – Politics and government – 1990–1995.*
3. Progressive Conservative Party of Ontario.
4. Electioneering – Ontario. I. Title.

FC3077.2.B55 1995   971.3'04   C95-932090-3
F1058.B55 1995

Dundurn Press Limited
2181 Queen Street East
Suite 301
Toronto, Canada
M4E 1E5

Dundurn Distribution
73 Lime Walk
Headington, Oxford
England
0X3 7AD

Dundurn Press Limited
1823 Maryland Avenue
P.O. Box 1000
Niagara Falls, N.Y.
U.S.A. 14302-1000

For my husband Dave and my sons Paul and Julian

For their patience and support

CONTENTS

ACKNOWLEDGMENTS

I wish to thank the *Toronto Sun* for the privilege of covering the 1995 Ontario election campaign. Portions of this book are reproduced with permission from columns that appeared in the newspaper during the election period.

I would also like to thank the many people who granted interviews for this book, including the premier and deputy premier. I would especially like to thank members of the Liberal campaign team who graciously agreed to be part of this book.

The publisher and I wish to thank the Progressive Conservative Party of Ontario for permission to use the cover photograph of Mike Harris.

We also want to thank Denis Drever, Leslie Pace, Gord Haugh, Deb Hutton, and Sean O'Shea for sharing their photographs.

Chapter One
Coronation to Revolution

Everyone predicted a coronation. Queen Lyn of the Liberals was supposed to sweep to power in Ontario's provincial election. With Jean Chrétien and his federal Liberals still getting record approval ratings, conventional wisdom said that McLeod would romp to victory on his coattails. Ontario wasn't supposed to turn right. Mike Harris wasn't supposed to be premier. Voters in the country's warm, fuzzy heartland were deemed too sophisticated, too socially concerned, just too darned nice to vote for Chainsaw Mike and his team.

Before the election, Harris and his rag-tag crop of Tories and their "Common Sense Revolution" were derided in the Ontario legislature as a steal from the U.S. right. Harris was portrayed as a Canadian Newt Gingrich who would slash and burn our most treasured social programs. They called him Mike the Knife, Newt of the North – any number of derisive epithets that were supposed to paint him in an extreme right corner. But while the Liberals and New Democrats were scoffing at his platform, Harris and his troops were criss-crossing the province at the grass-roots level, talking to people in town hall meetings from Kapuskasing to Cornwall to Windsor.

McLeod and her Liberals were sitting with a fairly consistent two-to-one lead in the polls throughout the fall and winter of 1994. By the spring of 1995 Harris was generally discounted as a serious contender in the election which everyone knew was just around the corner. However, the politically perceptive could see the signs. There was the Victoria-Haliburton by-election, which was called when New Democrat incumbent Dennis Drainville quit in disgust over his party's policy on casinos. The Tories swept in neophyte Chris Hodgson, who personifies the new breed of Conservative, in what proved to be a dry run of the 1995 election. Some saw the signs as far back as the day after the New Democrats came to power in 1990. It was apparent then, pundits claim, that Premier Bob Rae and his socialist government were inexperienced and lacked the political savvy to hang on to power for longer than one mandate. Besides, did Ontarians really understand what they had wrought in electing a socialist agenda? In their haste to spank a naughty David Peterson and his Liberal government for their arrogance, had Ontario voters opened up a whole can of socialist worms?

The final sign that the Liberals might not have a cakewalk in the 1995 provincial election came, surprisingly, in the federal election of October 1993, when Ontario voters returned 98 Liberals in 99 ridings. Astute observers pointed out that no matter what the polls said, when push comes to shove, Ontarians like to see diversity in their political representation. They rarely choose to have the same party govern them from Ottawa and Queen's Park at the same time.

It seemed impossible, but a small group of Tories believed they had a plan for Ontario. They were the ones who were left to pick up the pieces of a shattered provincial party. They were a small, shell-shocked group of generally right wing Conservatives who had kept the blue flame of Toryism burning after the cataclysmic upheaval of 1985. It was hard to believe that the once-mighty Tories had been reduced to a deficit-ridden rump, who could elect only a handful of members to a legislature which they had ruled as benevolent dictators for forty-two heady years. This small group of party loyalists had absolute faith not in the Big Blue Machine but in their ability to build their own, new political vehicle. They inherited a cranky old jalopy of a political party, stripped it of its excess baggage, gave it a new engine, and streamlined it for the 1990s. They even repainted it, subtly changing its color from Tory blue to a royal purple, which provides a richer hue for television.

But there was no magic bullet, no secret election formula to the Tory win. Moreover, there were no clever tricks by U.S. consultants. The Liberals were fixated on negative advertising and how to respond to it and even fearful of U.S. election consultant Mike Murphy. The Tories, meanwhile, plugged away for five years getting their message out, listening to grass-roots Ontarians, and formulating policy. By the time New Democrat Premier Bob Rae dropped the election writ on the desk of Lieutenant Governor Hal Jackman, on 28 April 1995, the Tory campaign was ending, rather than beginning.

They already had done their polling and listened to all the fears that were gnawing at the hearts of Ontarians. Their leader already had glad-handed across the province, talking to everyone from Bay Street CEOs to factory workers, to find out what they wanted from their government. More importantly, they took an immense gamble in releasing their policy document more than a year before the election call. It was an almost unheard-of election strategy. Liberals and New Democrats alike privately snickered and publicly ridiculed the Tories' bold plan – the "Common Sense Revolution" – which the Tories had distilled from all those town hall meetings and private dinners.

In the end, the strategy proved brilliant and unassailable. The Tories prescribed strong medicine for what ailed the province. In a scheme dubbed "workfare," Harris proposed that welfare recipients work for their benefits. And Ontario's benefits, which were 30 percent above the national average, would be rolled back to only 10 percent above what other provinces pay. As well, Harris vowed to end the New Democrats' new employment equity legislation that required employers to hire specifically targeted numbers of women and minorities. Another Tory promise was a pledge to cut taxes. In four and a half years of government, the New Democrats had increased taxes by $4 billion. Harris vowed to cut taxes by the same amount through a 30 percent cut in the provincial income tax rate.

Not surprisingly, his opponents jumped on that figure. McLeod declared that he was going to cut taxes – not the income tax rate – by 30 percent and that he was "wacky" for doing so.

On election day, Ontarians opened wide, said aaaah, and took their Tory medicine with a smile.

And the coronation became a revolution.

Chapter Two

A House Divided

Newly elected Premier Mike Harris planned the timing of his swearing-in ceremony carefully and with a sense of history. It was ten years exactly to the day – 26 June 1995 – that Liberal Premier David Peterson and his new government were sworn in on the lawn of Queen's Park, ending a forty-two-year Tory dynasty in Ontario. And it wasn't just the imagery of ten lost years that Harris was trying to depict. Within the PC party itself, things had come full circle. The decade had been far from wasted by the Tories. During those years, their party had been pulled apart and then rebuilt from the ground up.

By 1985, it was clear to some political observers that four decades of Tory rule were about to end. There was internal party strife, much of it coming from the Ontario Campus Progressive Conservatives in the persons of Tom Long and Tony Clement, who opposed what they saw as Red Tory policies – the SUNCOR bailout and full funding for separate schools. They bitterly denounced changes to the enforcement of the Ontario Human Rights Code tabled by Bob Elgie. The changes included the power to obtain material without a warrant and due process, which Long and Clement considered draconian, undemocratic, and certainly not particularly Progressive Conservative in nature.

The campus Tories wanted a discussion of these new policies, but they were shut out of the party's policy debates by the old guard. It was a defining moment for the campus Tories. They realized that the old-style Tories really didn't want a lot of discussion, and whenever there was dissent, they would simply shut it down. Eventually, the old guard relented – a little. But it was too late for Long and Clement and their allies, who realized that if the Tories were going to survive, the party had to be opened up and democratized.

And then came 1985 – the Tories' very own annus horribilus. It was a year of turmoil, pain, and enormous upheaval for the Conservatives. Premier William G. Davis – Smilin' Bill, Brampton Billy, one of the most respected politicians in Ontario – resigned at Thanksgiving 1984. He'd been leader and premier of the province since 1971, winning general elections in 1971, 1975, 1977, and 1981. (His second and third victories produced minority governments.) In 1983 and 1984, there was a "will-he-won't he" period during which many in the party urged Davis to take a run at the leadership of the federal Tories, to succeed Joe Clark. Davis ended all the speculation in October 1984, by resigning as party leader.

Immediately, the party was plunged into a feeding frenzy of two leadership contests within the same year. This proved both costly and divisive. Round one came in January 1985, which wasn't so much a political party choosing a new leader as it was an elite group of Conservatives anointing the next premier.

The party disintegrated quickly. Frank Miller, Dennis Timbrell, Larry Grossman, and Roy McMurtry squared off for the job. Miller won on the last ballot; Grossman was second. Miller called an election for May 1985 and the party dropped 20 seats. The New Democrats and Liberals ganged up on the government and defeated it on the Throne Speech vote. Miller resigned in August, and in November, the party endured another self-destructive leadership campaign.

"It was assumed we were electing a new premier. There was a lot of bitterness, a lot of division, a lot of fighting. And you had to go for the delegate spots – 10 delegate spots per riding," recalled David Lindsay, who is now Harris's principal secretary and one of the premier's closest confidants. Lindsay watched the whole debacle unfold as a junior party worker. It was, he remembered, like "family fighting against family." There were huge, internal battles. The party faithful fought over delegate spots and fundraising, and the leadership candidates fought to make commitments and promises. It took only twelve months for schisms and divisions to appear in the once-mighty PC party. Cracks and fissures opened up beneath their feet – and the Tories plunged downward.

"In those years, 1984-85, the party was tired. The leadership candidates didn't seem to be running on ideas, they seemed to be running on who best to continue the mantle," says Lindsay. "It wasn't really a rejuvenation. The new ideas weren't as forthcoming, or weren't sparking debate as much as asking who was best to maintain the power. Or who best to pick up the torch and carry the mantle of the Tory dynasty – as opposed to who is rejuvenating the party and bringing forth new ideas."

Tories wouldn't even accept the fact that Frank Miller had lost the election in 1985. After all, he had won 52 seats. David Peterson only had 48. They wanted to claim victory, but the Liberals and New Democrats had forged an agreement to bring down the government right after the Throne Speech. The Liberal-New Democrat accord shook the Tories right down to their Stanfield underwear. They were used to governing Ontario by holy writ. It was their divine right to occupy the plush offices on the second floor of Queen's Park. And how dare those upstart Liberals upset the natural order of things?

Miller put a sign on the door of the premier's office telling Peterson not to get too comfortable. "We'll be right back" was the sentiment. The Tories spent ten long years in the political wilderness, but on 8 June 1995, they honored that commitment.

In 1985, however, the Tories took on an unfamiliar role in the legislature. They sat in the Opposition with 52 seats, which went down to 51 when Bob Elgie took over the Workers' Compensation Board. A second leadership campaign started when Frank Miller resigned in the summer of 1985. Larry Grossman took a second run at the leadership, this time defeating Allan Pope and Dennis Timbrell.

In the meantime, the Tories had people on the Opposition benches in the legislature who had never been in that position before and didn't quite like the view. It's understandable. Leo Bernier, Dr. Bette Stephenson, Claude Bennett had sat around the cabinet table for ten years and simply weren't prepared for political obscurity.

Lindsay remembered one telling moment that happened in the dying days of the Miller government, shortly before the Throne Speech was voted down. It was Question Period, and the Liberals and New Democrats were giving Tory Dennis Timbrell a particularly tough time. Timbrell looked across the floor of the legislature and shouted back, "You guys are going to find it's a lot tougher to catch the spears than it is to throw them."

So the Tories found themselves in opposition, with no internal gyroscope to give them direction. They lost their identity. The natural ruling party was no longer ruling, and they felt that they had lost their raison d'être.

And then an odd notion dawned on the people of Ontario. David Peterson had been sworn in as premier of Ontario. There was a Liberal government at the Pink Palace, and the sky hadn't fallen. Imagine that, after forty-two years, another party could govern without the province collapsing – or so they thought.

In 1985, voters hadn't slam-dunked the Tories out of power. On the contrary, the Conservatives technically won the election. But once the electorate got a better look at the newly made-over David Peterson, with his trendy hairdo and stylish clothes, the new, trendy, and stylish voters in Ontario decided that they really preferred him and the Liberals to the stuffy old guard Tories.

By 1987, the voters were willing to do what they hadn't had the temerity to do in 1985 – they swept out the Tories and swept in the Liberals with a huge majority government.

Chapter Three

No Cents and Common Sense

There was good news and bad news for Brampton South MPP Tony Clement right after the 1990 election. The good news was that he'd been elected party president. The bad news came during his first day on the job, when he received a phone call from the party's chief financial officer.

"Congratulations on becoming party president," said the CFO. "I just want to let you know that we're $5.4 million in debt. That means before we pay a nickel on staff, before we pay a nickel on brochures, anything, we have to pay in interest $625,000 a year – $13,000 a week. And right now we have about $4,000 in the bank."

That was the financial state of the Big Blue Machine following the 1990 leadership campaign. Mike Harris had inherited a massive debt, racked up during all those leadership campaigns. After the fall election of 1990, things looked grim for the Tories. With the party consistently at 15 or 20 percent in the polls, the $5.4 million debt sat like a huge boulder on a road, blocking any chance the Tories may have had of rejuvenating themselves.

That's when Mike Harris made one of the toughest decisions of his political career – he shut down party headquarters. It was the only thing the party could do, but it meant that the once mighty Big Blue Tory Machine of Ontario no longer existed. Traditional Conservatives were aghast. It was unthinkable for them; it was akin to the Albany Club running out of twelve-year-old scotch. The Tories had no party headquarters and no paid political staff.

But the hole in the bank was only the tip of the iceberg. Not only were the Tories financially bankrupt, but they were also fresh out of new ideas. Long-time Harris friend and confidant David Lindsay argued at the time that it wasn't just a financial problem – the party faced four deficits. "The easiest to measure, because you have monthly financial statements, and the most visible and tangible was the financial deficit," Lindsay commented.

"Secondly, organizationally there was a deficit," he said. "There weren't very many people involved in the party any more. They had left for myriad reasons. Some joined the party because of power, some joined because of philosophy, some joined for many reasons and we'd lost of lot of those reasons and they left."

The third deficit was one of intellect. There was a distinct lack of ideas. There was hardly any ability to develop policies, and almost no knowledge of how to govern. All the people with experience in government had gone, either to Ottawa, where the Tories were in power, or to the private sector. There were nothing and no one to stimulate new ideas within the party.

The fourth deficit was a strategic one. "Why are we in this business?" Tories asked themselves. Any private sector business, Lindsay pointed out, has a mission statement and strategic planning exercises that challenge workers to consider what service they provide or what product they sell. But Tories had lost their sense of direction, they no longer knew what they were about. And there was, Lindsay said, a great need to ask why the Tories were still there, in the political party business.

"Are we just in this to get the keys to the limousines, or are we really trying to provide good government. Or are we really just a patronage machine. What is the Progressive Conservative Party of Ontario?" These were some of the questions the Tories had to come to terms with.

The party had to start rebuilding systematically in all of those areas. And the first thing they did was go through exactly the kind of strategic planning exercise which private corporations go through when they have lost their rudder. They needed to identify opportunities, strengths, and weaknesses. They had to do some mission planning. So the Tories invited the party youth, campus clubs, women's groups, riding associations, fundraising people, and even staff at Queen's Park to participate in these strategic planning sessions.

Just as the management of Harvey's might sit down to figure out just how they can make the best darned hamburgers in town, or the folks at Tim Horton's might strategize on donuts, Ontario's Tories sat down to figure out what it was they were trying to deliver. And once they'd figured out where it was they wanted to be, they looked for ways to get there.

After months of agonizing, they put all the material together in their "Mission '97" statement, which they gave out to approximately 750 members at the party's general meeting in Windsor, in October 1992. And the "'97" part of the title wasn't a misprint. The Tories decided that their goal, their mission as a party, was not simply to get elected. They were building a model of good government for Ontario, a model which they wanted to apply two years after the next provincial election. "Mission '97" said in part: "We will build a safe and prosperous Ontario by: – adhering to the shared values based on individual rights and responsibilities, fairness and equality of opportunity'.' And it went on: "(by) Governing with responsive, competent and principled leadership (by) Implementing consistent, innovative and responsible policies."

Setting out a fairly straightforward structure for delegates to follow. "Mission '97" showed them how the party could rebuild. Moreover, the booklet elicited comments and suggestions from delegates on how best to implement the strategy, and it provided pages within the leaflet for party workers to respond to the mission statement. "Mike Harris and the steering committee, based on input from the party, decided they didn't want a statement that focused simply on the short term goal of getting elected, but one which reflected the longer term goal of governing Ontario. The action plans flowing from this mission statement should focus not only on getting elected but on how we will govern after that election," the booklet explained.

And this was a fairly revolutionary approach for the staid, some might say hidebound, Conservative party. It actually solicited open debate. Its stated goal was more than getting elected; it wanted to provide good and sound government.

The booklet went on to ask questions. "Articulating, communicating and integrating our shared values in everything we do is a strategic objective. How best can you do that in your riding and how should we as a party do it centrally?" Here, then, was the central office asking the advice of the ridings. It was quite a turnaround for the Tories.

It went on to ask about election strategy: "To implement our agenda, we must win the next election. A detailed election strategy must be developed and implemented. What five things must you and your local association do to achieve this objective? Remember we need money, organization and people to run a successful campaign."

And further, the document invited direct involvement from its members and asked for their input on policy and strategic initiatives.

Lindsay said that the change of focus – from winning the election to providing good government two years after the election – was crucial to restoring the heart and soul of the party. It restored its sense of raison d'être. "We concluded, as the Progressive Conservative Party of Ontario, that our job is not to win elections," Lindsay explained. "Our job is to provide good government. So the psychology changed. Once you've made that psychological switch in your mind, that we're not just here to rat on the government, or not here just to be a good opposition party or to win an election campaign, we're here to try to provide good government. To build a safe and prosperous society for Ontarians by adhering to certain values and principles. That's what we decided we wanted to be. And that sets your internal gyroscope. So now everything you do is to provide good government. Not just to get a headline in tomorrow's paper. Not just to embarrass the government."

And that was an ambitious goal for a third party with only 20 seats in the legislature.

Lindsay compared the process to a farmer plowing a field. "If you go down into the valley, and you haven't set that stake out far enough, you're going to lose your way. We set the stake out far enough – it was Mission '97, not Mission '95."

While all this was going on, David Lindsay, Tom Long, and

others set out to repair the intellectual deficit. They needed to bring new ideas into the party. Mike Harris, something of an outsider from North Bay, hadn't travelled in Bay Street circles, and he needed to understand that community. Harris is not a pinstripe Tory. He's not a part of the old school tie clan of Tories. He doesn't even pretend to be part of the corporate elite which the party has represented for a long time.

In 1992 and 1993, Tory insiders with help from John Craig Eaton, George Eaton, and Bill Farlinger of Ernst and Young introduced Harris to the movers and shakers and corporate elite of Bay Street. He needed them financially and intellectually.

Harris and the Tories set out on a voyage of business discovery, to find out what was on the minds of the Bay Street brokers. Within a year, Harris had attended fifty-two dinners, with an average of ten diners each, and discussed business with more than 500 of the province's most influential lawyers, CEOs, and business people. Harris would bounce ideas off them, seek their advice, and ask for feedback on a wide range of topics: the economy, changes in international finance, the business community, and computer technology. They'd discuss free trade, demographics, and education needs for training the workforce. It was a brilliant way to educate Harris on the business community.

But he still needed to get to know the average Ontarian – and this was key to the Tory strategy. Harris's people knew that there were a lot of small "c" conservatives out there. The problem was how to meet them and listen to what was on their minds.

In this respect, Lindsay stole a page out of Manitoba Premier Gary Filmon's book. Filmon was an old hand at inviting people to have "coffee and conversation with the premier." He liked to visit Manitoba's many small towns. In advance of his arrival, he would send out a few thousand invitations to the townspeople, telling them that the premier would be coming and asking them to drop by the Moose Lodge or the Legion Hall – wherever – to talk to him.

The Tories tried the same strategy, the only difference being that it's a lot easier to get people to come out for coffee with the premier than it is to get folk to drop by to chat with the leader of the third-place party. But all the same, they had a respectable show-ing at most of these gatherings. If they sent out 1,000 invitations, they'd get fifty to a hundred people. The numbers were hardly headline material, but these "town hall" meetings were a start, and they set the party back on the road to restoring its organizational deficit.

Money problems persisted, of course, although re-establishing Bay Street links helped things a little, and reaching out to the grass roots gave the party something of a boost. What sustained the party during the lean years was a database of 30,000 names. They were the names of little old ladies and regular folk from small towns across Ontario who still believed in conservative ideals and who would send in their $5, $10, or $100 cheques whenever the party sent out a begging letter. They were the people who kept them going.

Despite the image of the party being a bastion of big business and big money, it was essentially direct-mail campaigns to individ-uals that kept the blue Tory flame burning. Lindsay described the everlasting gratitude Harris and his followers have for those people. When the party was at the depths, both in poll numbers and in morale, they still had enough faith to dig deep into their pockets for a party which few critics believed would ever return to power.

Lindsay credited long-time Tory fundraiser Stuart Eagles with restoring Tory finances. Eagles, a retired Marathon Realty CN executive and a dollar-a-year volunteer for the Conservatives, went into the Tory fund office and slowly and systematically helped get fundraisers back on track. Eagles set a goal for himself to have 100 new corporate fundraisers, business people who would make cold calls or calls to their colleagues around Christmas time in order to get the year-end donation in.

It was tough sledding. Federal Conservative Prime Minister Brian Mulroney and his government had reached the nadir of their popularity. The words Progressive and Conservative were anathema to the country. It was not an easy time to raise funds for the party in Ontario. Polls at the time showed the Tories at 15 percent of popular support.

As things gradually started to brighten, the Tories began to hold fundraising dinners again. They hadn't done those for two or three years because the infrastructure that supported them had disappeared. Some old friends of the party, such as Joe Barnicke, John Craig Eaton, and Stuart Eagles, pitched in. "They obviously didn't do it because it was going to benefit them in any way," recalled Lindsay. "It was for the good of the party and to keep an old democratic institution like the Tory party of Ontario alive." These were the people who helped start up the fundraising dinners again.

By 1991-92, they were able to pay down $100,000 on the debt. It wasn't a lot, but it was a start. The debt now stood at $5.3 million. By closing down headquarters and firing staff, they had stopped the bleeding. They weren't adding to the debt. However, they had to raise $600,000 a year just to cover the interest payments.

That's where the direct-mail campaign came in. That money kept their heads above water, and the money Eagles raised through corporate canvassing and fundraising dinners went to pay down the principal on the debt. The next year the Tories were able to pay down $1 million, and the following year they paid down another $1 million. They had two years of million-dollar surpluses, and by year-end 1993 they were able to reduce the debt to $2.9 million. In 1994, while the Tories appeared on the surface to be languishing in the political wilderness as the third party, with only 20 members in the legislature, they raised more money than they ever had when they were the government.

Finally, they were in shape to face the election. They had money, they had ideas, they had people. Most importantly, they had redefined a new mission for themselves.

Chapter Four
Out of the Smoke

For forty-two years, the hardcore elite within the Conservative party had held several truths to be self-evident. The first was that God was most assuredly an Anglican. Many Tories were Anglican. In fact, the Anglican Church was known as the Tory party at prayer. It was the party that upheld the British traditions of God, Queen, and country. The second truth was that the premiership of the province was a Tory birthright. With government in both heaven and earth pretty well sewn up, it came as an enormous shock then for the Tories suddenly to find themselves in opposition, confused and rudderless in a great political tide that was sweeping past them with enormous force.

David Lindsay, Mike Harris's principal secretary, described the process the party went through in the wake of their devastating electoral loss as the kind of grieving process people go through when someone close to them dies. After the 1987 Liberal sweep, the Tories found themselves going through denial – the "We'll be right back" stage. And then there was the anger – the "You guys will find those spears harder to catch than it is to throw them" kind of statement. Then there was the grief – Tories went down to 17 members, unheard of for Ontario PCs.

Finally, there was rejuvenation. It was a long, searing process, but in the end it paid off. And the first step back onto the right road was the decision not to have another leadership campaign too soon. Instead, they appointed an interim leader. Being Tories, of course, they had to fight over who would be the caretaker. But the decision was inspired. The genial Andy Brandt, now the head of the Liquor Control Board of Ontario, was just the person to start the healing.

"Andy, because of his personality – he's an affable, jovial, friendly and nice guy – helped with that grieving process," Lindsay recalled. "He was good, he was humorous, he played a role in soothing people."

Meanwhile, the party started to restructure itself and change the way it did things. First of all, it was driven by factional rivalries. The people who were left came to be known by the person they had worked for in this or that leadership campaign. It was as if all the Tories had a name stamped on their foreheads. She worked for Grossman. He's a Timbrell man. Look out, here comes a bunch of Miller people. The Tories finally realized that they were in need of an enormous amount of internal healing and also that they had to bring fundamental changes to the party, so that they would never end up in the same state they were in after the 1987 election.

The first and most important thing the party did was change the nature of leadership conventions. The party that was wracked with rivalries, that had been through two horrendous orgies of back-biting, reformed the way it chose its leaders. It wasn't easy. Getting two Tories to agree on anything can be difficult. Persuading two-thirds of their members to make a constitutional change that would open up the party and democratize it was extremely difficult, but a determined group that included Tom Long and Tony Clement managed to persuade the party to go to a one-member, one-vote process. The Parti Québécois already used such a system to choose its leader, but the process was revolutionary to Ontario. The Conservatives were the first provincial party in English-speaking Canada to adopt it. The days of arm twisting delegates in smoke-filled backrooms were over.

Clement, assistant principal secretary to Mike Harris, was at the vortex of the radical transformation that took place within the party, and he co-chaired the constitutional committee that came up with the one-member, one-vote idea.

"That process allowed a person like Mike Harris to be selected. It pushed down the authority and responsibility for selecting a leader to every member of the party, rather than an elite core of people at some arena in Toronto or Ottawa deciding. It was every member of the riding deciding in his or her own constituency," Clement recalled.

That was the beginning of the restructuring process. More than any other date – 12 May 1990 – is key to the Tory win of 1995. That was the day Mike Harris became leader of the Tory party, and he couldn't have been elected leader without the one-member, one-vote system. And the Tories would never have won in 1995 if Mike Harris hadn't become leader in 1990. He was an outsider; he wasn't a member of the party elite; and he didn't hold enough sway among the ruling clique to get the nod. Yet he received 55 percent of the votes to beat London North MPP Dianne Cunningham. Once the party dragged the leadership contest out of the smoky backrooms, where big money bought delegates and votes, the reform and rebuilding could start.

The new system was quite simple – everyone had a vote, from the farmer in Grey County to the Bay Street moneyman to the Young Progressive Conservative kid in Don Mills. Everyone had an equal say in the outcome of the leadership race.

Harris never forgot that he was the first person elected leader on the one-member, one-vote system. As a backbencher, he saw that a small group in cabinet made all the decisions. Changing the party structure and having more people involved created a new psychology within the party, and he was very much in tune with it.

Harris had little time to savor his leadership triumph. During the last week of July 1990, David Peterson called a snap election for September. The Tories were left scrambling to find 110 candidates, write a party platform, raise money, and develop a campaign strategy. They had seventy-five days.

But if David Peterson had hoped to catch the Tories off guard, the ploy backfired. This time it was the Liberals who were decimated. Mike Harris and the Tories did much better than anyone had predicted or expected. Lindsay, backroom strategist John Laschinger, Leslie Noble, who worked for Laschinger and who became co-chair of the 1995 campaign, Mitch Patten, Tom Long, and a handful of other allies all pitched in to do the best they could under the circumstances. Some pundits gleefully predicted that Harris wouldn't be returned in his own riding of Nipissing. In fact, it was Peterson who lost his seat. Harris was easily re-elected, and the Tories ended up with 20 seats, which they rightfully saw as a great victory. At least they now had a solid base in the legislature on which to build for the next election.

Chapter Five

Don't Underestimate This Guy

T here is one thing which you hear consistently from those who know Ontario's new premier, and it is a warning. Do not ever underestimate Mike Harris.

Many people, friends and foes alike, have done so throughout his career and lived to rue the day. Harris may not dazzle you with rhetoric or repartee, but he is nevertheless shrewd and tough, letting nothing escape his eagle eye. Commentators have noted that his hunched, shambling gait tends to give him downcast or a humble look. But he is very much his own man.

In underestimating Mike Harris, the Tory candidate for the premier's job, the Liberals sank their own campaign ship in 1995. Before the election, their staffers would tell you that Harris was going to lose it. He wouldn't stand up to the immense scrutiny that takes place in campaigns. He would lose his temper and collapse. It was all nonsense, of course. He went from strength to strength, staying calm and cool and making only a couple of minor gaffes. Tom Long, campaign co-chair, claimed that aside from Harris's obvious blunders on university tenure and the Windsor casino, he was brilliant.

"He was like a laser, locking on to issues. I have never seen a leader as disciplined in getting his message across. He was amazing. He carried this thing in terms of getting the message across. We tried to provide him with visually interesting and novel ways of delivering the message."

And there is, in some quarters, the feeling that this victory was somehow a fluke, a come-from-behind win orchestrated by a bunch of clever strategists who knew all the tricks and who somehow managed to hoodwink vast portions of the electorate into voting for their guy. But it was no fluke. Harris was personally involved in all aspects of the campaign. Key members of his team will tell you that his fingerprints are all over the Common Sense Revolution. He couldn't be tripped up during the election because he knew the platform inside out. And he knew it because he helped to draft large portions of it. The real success story in the Tory election victory is the focus Mike Harris brought to it, according to Leslie Noble, the campaign's other co-chair.

"He's a true leader. He consults, he listens, but he makes a decision. And when he goes forward, there is no wishy-washyness about him. He has the courage of his convictions.

"When I first got involved with Mike Harris as a politician it was shortly after Larry Grossman resigned and we talked about whether he would become leader of the party and what needed to be done and what was the right way of doing that.

"From that minute forward, what I have learned is that he is one of the best strategic thinkers of any of the politicians that I have ever worked for. He is dedicated beyond belief and has the ability to see the long term, to view things in the long range, and he is patient enough that he will do what needs to be done to do it right, as opposed to looking for the quick fix."

It was that kind of drive that compelled him to push for the democratization of the party with the one-member, one-vote leadership contest. Harris recognized that the Tories had lost touch with the public and even their own party. The people who actually went out and worked on campaigns and knocked on doors had little input into what the party did once it was elected to Queen's Park. That's what Harris wanted to change, said Noble. He wanted to reconnect the party with its workers.

"When you don't have that kind of input, what's to motivate you to go door-to-door, to get involved? And I don't care what anyone says, volunteers are still the lifeblood of any political party and without them you die a fast death.

"He was the first leader to recognize that we had done wrong as a party. That there wasn't this divine intervention that would happen and return the rightful governing party to its place, which seems to be the attitude that a lot of people in our party had for five years – that the voters made a mistake.

"The voters never make a mistake," Noble asserted.

Harris recognized that the Tories themselves had bungled things, and he was prepared to take the party by the reins and drive it in a new direction. Some say that Harris won the party leadership because no one else wanted it. "I won the leadership because when I announced, I saw a strategy there to go and win – whether there were 50 people running or one," Harris said.

When Harris became leader in 1990, he wasn't prepared for the election call that came six weeks later. People who worked on that campaign remember how everything was done on the fly. Harris was often up at 3 a.m. writing speeches. He made a good showing, better than anyone predicted, but it just wasn't there for the Conservatives.

On the subject of the 1995 campaign, there persists a stubborn belief out there that his team won it for him, a theory which simply isn't true but points to a tendency in people to underestimate Harris and ridicule his beliefs. Harris agrees that the campaign was a good, well-thought-out one, but he's also quick to point out that it wasn't something that happened in the last three weeks of the campaign.

"It started two years ago," he said. "Those who were shocked and surprised really misread the public, or didn't understand it, including pollsters who asked the wrong questions or misinterpreted the results of what they got. It's not that they didn't get the right answers back, but they weren't asking the right questions. Or they were taking the results of what they were asking and drawing the wrong conclusions. I said this for a long time. It wasn't just rhetoric.

"The other thing was, we gave you the whole campaign, to the public and to the opposition fully a year before the election. It was the Common Sense Revolution. I guess the underlying theme, the key part of the strategy, was that we'd actually said the same thing for a whole year – unheard of in politics. The public didn't expect politicians to be consistent from one day to the next or one week to the next, let alone one mandate to the next – they'd been burned so many times."

The electorate has become cynical over the past fifteen or twenty years. It's a cynicism brought about by a succession of popularity poll politicians, who say one thing during an election and do something entirely different once they're elected.

"There's no question part of the strategy was to put the platform out a year ahead to be confident enough that we'd done enough listening and consultation and then we'd stick to it," Harris added. "And that, in and of itself, would be a great asset."

It was a strategy that was perfect for the times. And it was one which the Grits just didn't seem to grasp.

"The Liberal strategy seemed to be, 'Well, we'll wait as long as we can. And then we'll do the Red Book.' And it was the old politics. And there was no room out there in Ontario for the old politics," Harris said.

A cynical electorate chose Mike Harris because he was consistent, because what he said had a ring of truth to it. It was a message that was reinforced by Bob Rae and his campaign. Before the election, the New Democrats criss-crossed the province doling out money in a last-minute attempt to shore up support. And then Rae turned around completely during the election and said that he couldn't promise anything – least of all a tax cut.

"We were helped by the fact that Rae had a record that he said this and he didn't do it. He promised all the spending for three months and then he called the election and said, 'Hey, I'm not going to promise anything.' People didn't buy it. They weren't going to buy it anyway. But the main opposition was the Liberal Party, and the Liberal Party did not present that image."

Harris said that McLeod's apparent flip-flop on same-sex spousal benefits was devastating to her leadership image. He pointed out that during the by-election in St. George-St. David, where there is a large gay population, she had pledged to support the New Democrats' same-sex spousal benefits legislation. But when it appeared that her stand wasn't popular in other parts of the province, she backed away from that commitment. While the

Liberals maintain that it was the addition of adoption rights to the bill that made it unacceptable to their leader, the issue came back to haunt them again and again.

Harris went on: "Here was a leader who was not consistent, who was prepared to let us make all the tough decisions and three months after we took them, if the public liked them, if the polls said it was a good thing, they said, 'All right, us too.' And so we were helped by the fact that if you accept the fact that Rae wasn't going to get re-elected, it was a choice between Mike Harris and Lyn McLeod. If leadership was the issue, and it was part of it, then we were consistent and she wasn't. And it was a pretty clear choice.

"That was the first sign to us and to the public and the media and they asked, 'Does this leader stand for anything? Does she really believe in anything?'"

It wasn't even a question of same-sex benefits. That wasn't an issue in the campaign. It was the manner in which the Liberals were perceived to have used a minority group to their political advantage in a by-election, only to abandon them when the issue later proved – or was thought to have been proved – unpopular. And Harris reiterated that he doesn't believe same-sex benefits are even a top priority for many members of the gay community. "They have other concerns in life," he said.

"It was part of the fact that you didn't get to know Mrs. McLeod as a person of conviction, who believed in something or who stood for something and said, 'This is why I want to be premier.'" Harris added that it's the same problem that doomed federal Tory leader Kim Campbell in her catastrophic run in 1993.

"Kim Campbell had the same problem. I still don't know what she stands for – and the results of the election showed that. If you look at the last federal election, they went in almost even. Jean Chrétien was in fact less popular than Kim Campbell.

"I still think Kim Campbell could have won that election. I think if she had demonstrated a toughness, a belief in something – 'Here's what I stand for, and I'm a leader.' But we never saw that. I didn't see it in the leadership. I didn't see it in the campaign." Harris acknowledged that the Brian Mulroney factor, coupled with a good Liberal campaign, may have combined against Campbell, but he believed that the 1993 federal election didn't have to be the rout it turned into. The federal Liberals, he said, ran the right campaign for the time. They offered the country hope – and Campbell didn't.

Looking at the devastation of the federal election, the Ontario Tories realized that they too had to offer solutions and a viable alternative to the status quo. They too had to offer hope that these things could be done. "The mood wasn't just for change. The mood also was for trust, and believability and consistency, and to stand for something – and Ms. Campbell didn't do that and we did."

Harris said that he knew, even before the polls started to show the Tories catching up to the Grits, that voters were starting to get his message.

"The polls came after the sense that you had out there ... the crowds, within two weeks, were doubling. It may not have been huge, but it was twenty-five to fifty or fifty to a hundred, comparable riding to comparable riding. We were getting thumbs up from truck drivers on the highways, you could sense that, you could feel that. The polls actually turned a little faster than we thought they would.

"We were operating under the premise that it would all happen in the last ten to fourteen days. People had not made up their minds. There was either a very high undecided factor or they'd parked their votes with the Liberals because they liked the Liberal Party better than they liked the PC party, but we were confident that that didn't matter. They weren't voting party any longer in this province. This was a wide-open election for us."

The polls showed that there was no place for Bob Rae to go on things like credibility and believability, opening the way for Harris and the Tories.

"I know what that's like. I looked at the believability and the credibility of Mike Harris and the Ontario PC party in 1990. There was no room there," Harris recalled. "There was lots of room to attack the government and create doubts about David Peterson, but no room to show they were going to trust us. So that's what Rae was facing. We knew this thing was winnable. I'm a very confident person, and I felt confident that we could win.

"I knew we could lose too. If we didn't execute properly, if we weren't able to get our message out. If the Liberal Party, particularly, was able to confuse our message, so that people didn't trust us, or if they were able to present something. Although increasingly pre-writ, it became obvious that they weren't going to follow that strategy. That they were going follow what we thought they would do, which was the old Liberal strategy, which we didn't think would work.

"The Red Book really reinforced that. We said, 'Boy, they're doing exactly what we said they would do,'" Harris added. In fact, the Grits played into the Tory hands all along. The Grits would blanket Tory policy. The Tories would take a stand, the Grits would tentatively test the waters and three months later come out with a similar policy.

The Tories jumped in ahead of the Liberals with the release of the Common Sense Revolution, more than a year before the election writ was dropped. When the Grits attacked it, the Tories knew that Lyn McLeod and company would live to regret it. And indeed it turned out that the Liberals came up with policies remarkably similar to the Common Sense Revolution, which they had ridiculed since its unveiling. To compound their problems, the Liberals had talked so tough on the CSR, it would be virtually impossible for them to blanket or smother it in the election.

"In the Red Book, they tried to blanket us, plus they tried to be Bob Rae, plus they tried to fund subways. We felt really good there. It was exactly the kind of campaign we thought they were going to run," Harris said.

And, despite a pledge to balance the budget, the Liberals promised all kinds of big ticket items which voters knew they could never deliver. Even the federal Liberals were talking fiscal restraint. Federal Finance Minister Paul Martin brought down a cut-and-slash budget in the spring which received widespread public support. Voters had started to realize that you can't have everything. Yet Lyn McLeod and the Liberals reverted to the old promise-you-anything type of platform.

"How can you commit to build four subways when even the TTC and Metro, who are usually the ones lobbying for these things, are saying, 'We can't afford four.' That just doesn't add up," Harris commented.

Harris remembered the reaction to McLeod's announcement that the Liberals planned to extend the GO Transit service to Peterborough.

"We said fine, we've got a good shot at Peterborough now. The people in Peterborough were saying, 'We understand, you can't afford to do that.' That was the mood out there, they knew that.

"There were a lot of people who voted for us who liked the idea of a tax cut but really deep down inside said, 'I don't think he can do it.'" Harris said that he's still absolutely committed to the first part of his 30 percent cut in the provincial income tax rate, and he is expected to make the cut in his first budget.

Then there was the debate. As in all such televised set-tos, the strategy was not necessarily to win. It was sufficient not to lose. Going into the debate, Harris knew that holding his own was pretty well all he could count on. Bob Rae, the Rhodes scholar, the able debater, the person with the quick wit and the clever turn of phrase, would likely win it from the academic point of view. And both Rae and Harris had to be careful not to be seen to be ganging up on McLeod, the woman who was a rookie at these things and therefore might be viewed as an underdog.

Harris entered the debate without worrying about the winners and losers. He was determined to talk to the people, and that's exactly what he did. At times during the debate, he looked straight into the camera and talked directly to the audience on issues which they had raised with him in his endless meetings with people across the province.

Curiously, the media generally concluded that the debate was a tie, and they gave a win to McLeod by default. In fact, she turned people off in droves, and focus groups recorded few negatives for Harris.

"It's a tough thing to evaluate, political debates," Harris said. "They seem to be measured on the debating society rules – Western vs. Queen's or Harvard vs. Cambridge – but that's fine for that measure. But that's not what you're after. You are in people's living rooms. What do they think of you?"

So why did Harris and the Tories appeal to so much of the electorate during the 1995 election? Did they really just happen on some issues – the hot buttons we heard so much about during the campaign – or was it a result of something far deeper?

"I think it was going out and actually listening to what people had to say," said Harris. "Matching that up with what we believe, and we may have heard some things that we fundamentally didn't agree with, but they were few and far between.

"Testing your own instincts and your gut and what you heard from people in the coffee shops and donut shops and town hall meetings, that was actually more reflective than what the so-called 'elites' were saying – 'Ontario is not like Alberta, we're not like the United States, we're middle of the road.' And of course the middle has moved so far in the last ten years that they were out to lunch on that.

"And trusting that was key – that what you heard was actually the middle of the road. That's what Ontario was thinking, that's what they were concerned about.

"There were a number of areas in that. Preston Manning had tapped in to some and others had tapped in to paying your own way."

Harris said that, strange though it may sound, the paying-your-own-freight philosophy is akin to an environmental mindset that wants to save the planet. It is similar to the strong emotions evoked during the great fish battle with Spain in the spring of 1995. But people want to save not just the fish and the rivers and the trees of this country. They want to preserve the economy and hand it on to their children and grandchildren debt-free.

"The very strong environmental movement of 'don't destroy this planet, don't create this factory for jobs today that means there's nothing here for our kids tomorrow' got translated fiscally. 'Don't spend my kid's money.' It's the same principle. And so it got translated into finances – balance the books, pay your own way. This borrowing money is immoral, it's wrong, it's taking away from your kids. That was very strong out there – to balance the books and to be fiscally responsible.

"What else was out there was a recognition – and it was after the fact, it was after the government tried to do all these things – that government can't do them very well. So not only can you not afford them, but you can't do them very well."

A good deal of this attitude crystallized around the photo radar vans that had mushroomed on the province's highways and had become a flash point for anti-NDP hatred.

"It was very strong. People were saying 'Get out of my face. I don't want any more inspectors. I don't want any more photo radar vans. And business people complained about the forms and the inspectors and the conflicts and taxation. We listened to them and we said, 'That's exactly what we believe.' So we can go fight for what we believe in with a great deal of confidence that this is what the people want to too. And it wasn't rocket science.

"People will tell you that there were these hot buttons – employment equity was a hot button. Welfare was a hot button. There were lots of them. What we said was that with the limited amount of dollars we have in this campaign you have to focus on one or two or three issues at the most and if you go beyond that in your advertising or in your focus, the message gets lost and it gets confusing."

And Harris knew that it would be a rocky row to hoe. There were other hot buttons out there that they could have pushed, but the three major ones – employment equity, welfare, and high taxes – fit in perfectly with Tory beliefs.

"We said, here are some. We're going to focus on them. We're going to stick to them. These are ones that are consistent with what we believe in, that we have fought for – that in some cases people have been afraid to talk about because they're afraid of being labelled. A case in point is employment equity.

"I think the public had had enough of all this political correctness. I think it was important, though, that we had gone through that. If you believe in something, you stood for it and you're prepared to fight for it – or get out. That was our attitude."

Chapter Six

Beyond the Big Blue Machine

Characterized as somewhat of an outsider by some of those closest to him, Mike Harris responds that he has never felt like an outsider. But he is not from the old Bay Street Tory crowd; nor is he one of the elite, Upper Canada College blue-bloods usually associated with the old-style party.

Harris was born in Toronto in 1945. Shortly afterwards his family moved north, to Callander, which is perhaps more famous as the birthplace of the Dionne quintuplets. His family operated small businesses. His dad gave up a successful welding supply company to take a flyer on a small business in the north. During the election, Harris was fond of telling how his parents, Dean and Hope Harris, had followed their dream and invested in a small tourist camp. The entire family worked hard to keep the dream on an even keel. Harris taught golf and skiing, while his mom cleaned cabins.

Harris went to Laurentian University and teachers college, and he eventually found a job teaching math in North Bay. In 1980, he was stricken with the mysterious Guillaine-Barre disease, a viral condition that attacks the nerves of the spine, and he was confined to a wheelchair for a brief period. But he was up and well enough to run in the 1981 provincial election. He confounded the pundits by breaking the twenty-two-year Grit stranglehold on Nipissing riding. Harris was a backbencher in the Bill Davis government, and he later served as minister of natural resources and Tory House leader.

His greatest skill as a leader, in the opinion of his colleagues, is his ability to pick exactly the right person out of a crowd and put him or her into a job in which they'll flourish and shine. And if you ask anyone on his campaign team – David Lindsay, Tom Long, Alister Campbell, Leslie Noble – what it was about their campaign that made it successful, they will tell you with one voice that it was Mike Harris. He may inspire Chainsaw Mike and Mike the Knife epithets among his opponents, but in his supporters he inspires absolute and complete loyalty. He also has an ability to bring warring sides together. That is a vital asset in a party that has been riven asunder by divisive leadership politics. Harris said that he has never viewed himself as belonging to one or other faction of the party.

"There are always factions in any family, or any business, or any party, I guess. I was certainly attracted to the party provincially because of an admiration for Bill Davis. But I have never felt shut out. When I was first elected, I worked my way through the ranks. I was never one who felt I should be in cabinet ahead of this or that person."

However, he has particularly harsh words for several of the power brokers within the party, such as Senator Norm Atkins, and blames people such as Atkins for some of the schisms within the Tory ranks. He remembers 1985 and the two leadership campaigns as a time of bitter division. He supported Frank Miller.

"That was my first real taste of party politics that was divisive. It was really rather bitter and I didn't like that. I supported Miller.

"There may be some who felt 'the Miller supporters are them and this is us' and vice versa," he recalled. "And I resented that. I didn't think it needed to be that way. If there's a downside to my experience with the PC party, it was the leaderships and how we refused to respect individuals' rights to make decisions on leadership selection.

"I lost a couple of good friends in my own riding because we had a disagreement over whether we would go with whatever Norm Atkins said. That might be construed negatively ... but it is a negative comment. I resented the fact that somebody said, 'This is who you support' and he [Atkins] at that time seemed to have that kind of control.

"I had people within my riding who, if Norm Atkins said, 'This is it,' that was it, 100 percent with blinkers on, and 'Anyone who doesn't agree with us, including Harris, is an outsider.'

"I almost had the feeling that if Norm called the following day and said, 'No, that's not the way,' they'd all say, 'Oh, okay.' I couldn't understand that. I'm a much more independent thinker."

It was his first party split, and it cut him to the quick. And it's partially why Harris was so much in favor of the one-member, one-vote system of choosing leaders.

"I was a very strong supporter of one-member, one-vote to change the way we select leaders – to avoid this kind of power and brokerage politics and the bitterness that can come from the aftermath of it.

"It was partially, too, how long it was. This unofficial leadership race went on too long, because we weren't sure when Davis was going to go. Before I was elected in 1981, they were lining up, understandably, and people were on unofficial campaign teams for two or three years. That's a long time.

"I didn't feel like I was an outsider at any particular point in time. I didn't draw any lines. I didn't think there were any camps within the parties. But others did. So as a result of that I was labelled as a Miller guy, so therefore I'm not a Grossman guy, or whatever else was there."

Those wounds have all healed, Harris said, and those who can't put things in the past have moved on to other things. And Harris added that while he didn't support Grossman in either of the leadership races, afterwards he and Grossman worked closely together. During the one-member, one-vote leadership campaign, which made Harris leader, both he and London North MPP Dianne Cunningham were able to garner support from all camps within the party. In some ways, this set the healing process in motion.

Those who know the party and Mike Harris stressed how central Harris was to the success of the party's platform. MPP Tony Clement, who was party president, spent several years as assistant principal secretary in Harris's office.

"You have to understand Mike is very much in charge," Clement remarked. "He was the one who set the direction. He was the one who pushed the limits and challenged the assumptions. He was the guy who did that. And none of this would have been possible without him."

Harris has a crystal clear way of looking at problems and cutting to the heart of an issue. Clement brought up the story of Peter North, the one-time NDP renegade who, in his search for a new political home, flirted with the idea of joining the Tories. There was animated discussion within Harris's office and the whole party about what to do with North. They wanted to deal with him fairly and remain true to their own principles. After all, Clement pointed out, "It's not every day an NDP member wants to become a Tory."

A hawks-versus-doves scenario emerged within the party. The hawks or hardliners took the position that under absolutely no circumstances should they allow the Elgin MPP, who'd been involved in a slightly unsavory episode, to join the party. North had baggage, and he didn't represent their fundamental Tory values. The doves countered by saying that he should be allowed in. He would be one extra member for the beleaguered Tories, he represented an area where the party wanted to be strong in the upcoming election, and if North was comfortable with becoming a Progressive Conservative, they saw no reason to say no.

Faced with two groups tugging away at the people closest to him, Harris came up with the only solution that satisfied everyone. He said that a decision could not be made by a handful of people in the leader's office. "It isn't our decision to make," Harris told the two warring factions. He insisted that the decision had to be made by the local riding association, since they were the people who would have to live with it. No one within the party had thought of that solution. Before Harris, such decisions had always been made by the party's inner circle, and it didn't occur to anyone, except their leader, to ask the people most directly affected.

So the Tories went back to North with a message that said, "Love to have you, but you'll have to get the endorsement of the riding association."

"Peter wasn't sure he'd get it," Clement recalled. "He didn't want to risk being rejected and eventually decided to run as an independent." It was an astute decision on North's part. He was re-elected.

Clement mentioned the appointment of Tom Long as campaign co-chair as indicative of Harris's management style. The choice of Leslie Noble as the other co-chair met with little opposition and was deemed by most party insiders to be a wise choice. But there was some uncertainty about Long, who was seen to be at the extreme right of the party.

Harris canvassed widely within the party for opinions. He talked to a variety of people, from all geographic and ideological points within the party. "He will talk to John Tory, he'll talk to Tom Long. He'll talk to Jean Charest, he'll talk to Preston Manning," said Clement. It is this broad consultative style that allows him to defuse controversy about often provocative decisions.

Harris spent a long time working on the decision to appoint Long. In 1993, people within the party were pushing Harris to appoint a campaign chairman. The Liberals had one, they reasoned, why not the Tories? But Harris wasn't ready. It wasn't until January 1994 that he finally settled for Long. He went through a very thorough process of advice-giving and consultation to come up with Long's name. And the time and effort paid off. The campaign team which seemed at first so disparate in fact worked together like a charm. And the person who can take credit for that is Mike Harris, all the team members said.

Apart from the chauffeur-driven limousine and the basketball court-size office, just how has life changed for Harris? According to Harris himself, "It's a weighty responsibility, no matter how much you anticipate it. It's a pretty awesome experience being here. Seeing how people respond to you differently is a bit of a surprise. It's not – if you actually think of it in logical terms – just that someone's going to return your phone call a little faster if you're premier than if you're leader of the Opposition and the polls say you are never going to get anywhere.

"It's been overwhelming actually, some of that response. Also, a little bit of the expectation that you're a different person." Harris said that people don't actually come right out and say, "Boy, you're a lot smarter now that you're the premier," but he senses from the different types of questions which he's been fielding that there's that kind of a sentiment out there.

"I'm no smarter or stupider than I was the day before the election."

And Harris has been surprised by friends who ask what to call him now that he's premier. "Whatever you called me before," he tells them.

Chapter Seven

Just Call Me Janet

One thing reporters quickly learned about Janet Harris was that she is a political wife like few they've seen before. She's neither cool and aloof, nor a shrinking violet clinging meekly to her husband. An attractive, strawberry blonde, Janet is witty and down to earth. She is forthright and has a delicious sense of humor. She dresses comfortably, rather than to a tee, and enjoys a good laugh. Occasionally, those laughs are at husband Mike's expense.

In an interview after the election, she said with a wicked chuckle, "I'm the one with the common sense. He's the one with the long-term financial outlook and budgeting. He's good at that long-term stuff, the things down the road. I'm good with the day-to-day stuff."

Like her husband, Janet Harris grew up in a family in which the kids were expected to help in the family business. They ran a dairy, and they were all on call, even after hours, to make a late delivery. "We could hardly wait until we were sixteen and could jump in the truck and take a delivery at ten o'clock at night," she remembered. It wasn't the kind of work for clock-watchers. "That's really good training and I think it's also good for learning common sense," she continued. "You learn common sense. You're not born with it – the practical things of getting work done. We never turned around to see who might do the job. If the job needed to be done and you were there, then you did it."

And she took credit for bringing out the kinder, gentler side of Mike Harris.

"I've attempted to make Mike a little bit more romantic, a bit more compassionate, although I also think the job has made him more compassionate and tolerant of other people's feelings. I've always said politics is really good for him in getting him to mature. But some of that has come from me, too. I'm more sensitive."

Even after a long and sometimes bitter campaign, in which her husband was often characterized as mean-spirited and hard-hearted, Janet said that she wasn't angry, only a little frustrated at some of the mud that was hurled at Harris.

"He has that kind of confidence, an inner strength, if you like," she said. "He's not a person who goes around defending himself. He's so positive and he's always taken the high road to things and been able to say, 'Well there will be people who will criticize, but the majority of people will hear my message and know what the other person says isn't right.'"

Janet confessed to being a political cartoon junkie. She gets a laugh out of some of the caricatures of her husband, even ones that are grotesquely unflattering. She's not quite as forgiving with the written word. If she knew that a story was going to be unfair or overly harsh in its criticism of her husband, she just didn't read it.

"Certainly some of the written stuff, some days, bothered me more than others and I didn't read the articles. I guess it was out of sight, out of mind. Not that that's the way you handle all problems. But some days, if I'd been off the bus for a few days and I felt maybe a little like I was missing the whole thing and missing Michael, then I maybe didn't read anything that day that sounded a little critical. I just didn't read it and that way I was able to cope."

She decorated the inside of the campaign bus with cartoons. "My album of the campaign is strictly cartoons. They're such a hoot. I think the more they exaggerate his features, the more real it is," she remarked. And she's disappointed that she can't get the *Toronto Sun* in North Bay and has to wait for the latest offering from Andy Donato to come up by mail.

"I think one of the problems in life is that we haven't been able to laugh at enough things – at ourselves." It was a sense of humor and the ability to laugh that kept her going on the gruelling campaign trail.

Harris was dogged by poverty protesters – Janet dubbed them the "Unfriendlies" – during the last couple of weeks of the campaign. "We'd get off the bus and say, 'Where are the Unfriendlies?'"

Reporters admired the gentle patience which she showed on the campaign trail, coping with her two very lively sons, three-year-old Jeffrey and ten-year-old Michael. Both boys spent time on and off the bus, and it was clear that they had a streak of pure mischief that kept mom hopping. Janet was quick to point out that at forty-six years of age she's an older mom, and the boys are a handful. Both of them are adopted, and Jeffrey has a mild case of cerebral palsy.

Several years ago, when Harris was absent from the legislature on numerous occasions, some of the media asked, "Where's Mikey?" It was even suggested by a few reporters that Harris, the leader of a third-place political party, preferred to spend his time on the golf course rather than at his desk. It transpired that the Harris family was going through a complicated adoption procedure when Jeffrey was a baby. It required a great deal of their time because of the youngster's CP. Harris chose not to publicize the procedure, preferring to keep his private life away from the prying eyes of the Queen's Park media.

Of course, Jeffrey was too young to understand the awesome responsibilities which his dad has assumed. Michael, on the other hand, was old enough to be a little ambivalent about his father, the premier of Ontario. "One day he's as proud as punch and thinks it's really neat. He's certainly aware of the responsibilities of the job. But then the next minute, he'd just as soon he'd be a nine-to-five, everyday, at-home kind of dad. He jumps from one to another," said Janet.

It was clear that Michael Harris Jr. sometimes resented the sudden spotlight that was thrust on his father. It was quite obvious to even the most casual observer that young Mike adored his dad and enjoyed a close relationship with him. He loved nothing more than to spend a day fishing with him. And it was plain that whenever hordes of media descended onto North Bay that Mike Jr. would have been just as happy if they'd left him and his dad alone. On election day he opted to go fishing with Janet's sister rather than face the committee room crowds.

"He'd had it by that point. He said, 'Enough,'" Janet recalled. "We had taken him on a two-day northern trip by plane, and that was fun." Unlike many political wives, Janet Harris got on well with most media types. They respect her good-natured, down-to-earth humor, while she was grateful for the way media on the tour helped her entertain Mike Jr. on the last gruelling leg of the campaign. "He got on particularly well with the Global guys we called the Oh-Ohs," she said of Global TV reporter Sean O'Shea and news cameraman Mike O'Drowsky. "They were really good with him and he spent a lot of time with them on the plane, and that was really neat."

Young Michael Jr. is definitely not the political type. Even though he's expected to make the obligatory appearances at various functions, Janet doesn't like to push him into the fray, particularly when there are noisy crowds, which tend to upset and frighten him. While the TV cameras searched for him in the committee rooms on election day, Janet admitted that it just wasn't something the youngster wanted to do. He was tired, and he knew that his dad was going to win. Although he was excited about it, he was not the kind of kid who can strike a cute pose and say all the right things for the cameras. Besides, he just wanted to go fishing.

"I think all you try to do is cope with the situation. And you try not to exploit them. It was important to me not to bring them through that crowd on election night."

Even mainstreeting is often not a place you want to be with children. There were usually noisy protesters. Some of them, Janet said, spit in Harris's face. That kind of behavior, combined with the crush of the media and party supporters, can produce a frightening experience for the children of politicians running in an election.

Of course, the mantle of premiership has changed Harris's life here in Toronto, but back in North Bay, he's still Mike to his friends, and Janet insists that's the way it has to be. She's determined that her husband's new job will have as little impact on her kids as possible. It's just a job, she said, and the kids need to keep that in perspective, even though it isn't always easy when their dad's away in Toronto most of the time and their lives are turned upside down when he's at home.

"But the good side is we get a lot of opportunities to go places and do things that a lot of kids will never do in their whole life. And that's the kind of thing I stress to him, and I don't know if he understands it, but I think he will when he's older. And perhaps he'll say, 'Mom was right about that. That was really neat that we got to do that.'"

Mike and Janet met at a waterski club in North Bay. "I pursued him," she said with a laugh. A mutual friend invited her across the lake to the club, she spotted Mike, whom she knew slightly from high school, and the rest is history. Janet remembered that she didn't really think that she was Mike's kind of woman, since he always preferred the sporty, athletic type. "I'm a great spectator," she said.

For Janet the key to the success of the campaign was Mike's ability to put the right person in the right job and to bring out the best in people. Harris has a grasp of the big picture, while she sometimes gets bogged down in detail.

"He's very good at looking at the whole picture of things," Janet pointed out. "I tend to get caught up in the exact moment, and he says, 'Well, stand back and look. Now what about this and this and this.' And I'll say, 'Oh, yeah, this does affect this decision.'"

The Harris' family pets include a large black Labrador dog named Fred – she's female – and a cat named Gordon. "I don't know where the names come from," Janet said with a sigh. "Young Mike liked the name Fred. His teddy bears were Fred, everyone was Fred. In fact, I'm glad he wore out of Fred, or little Jeffrey would have been Fred," she laughed. "Anyway, the animals seem to like their names."

The family may have to move to Toronto so the kids can see their dad more often, at least during the school term. Meanwhile, Janet Harris wants to keep her husband's new job as low key as possible.

"Our friends might joke and call him Mr. Premier, but he's still Mike, he still has to cut the grass and do things about the house. I want to try to keep our home life the same. I've always been one to say, 'It's just a job.' Not to demean the importance, of it, but for the children, I think that's very important, so they realize it is just a job. It's an important job. But it is just a job."

Chapter Eight

Dial 1-800-668-MIKE

On 21 January 1991, Bob Rae took a half-hour to discuss the dreadful state of finances in Ontario. This is serious, the Premier's Office warned the media. We need to consult with the people about what we're going to do. Normally, a dreary program telling viewers about the even drearier financial bog the province was in, narrated by the person who led us into the quagmire, wouldn't be a chart-topper. But a media flap about the TV show in the week leading up to its airing gave the program a high profile, and curious viewers tuned in to CFTO by the thousands to see what all the fuss was about.

It all started when Premier Bob Rae's communications aide John Piper decided to buy air time on CFTO-TV. He'd got a great deal, he said, a half-hour for $50,000, and the Liberals and Tories could have six and four minutes respectively at the end. Voices were raised in the media about why the premier was throwing away taxpayer dough to get across a message about fiscal restraint to the masses. After all, the province owned its own TV station – TVOntario. Why spend money in the private sector when we're all going to heck in a fiscal handcart anyway? Jumping on the bandwagon, the Liberals rather sanctimoniously told Piper that they wouldn't be part of the program if it was going to cost taxpayers money. They backed out.

At this point, David Lindsay, a close friend of Mike Harris and now his principal secretary, phoned Piper and said that if the Liberals didn't want the time, the Tories would take all ten minutes and they'd cut the government a cheque for the air time. Piper wasn't thrilled; nor were the Liberals.

In the end, the TV station management donated the air time, and all three parties jumped back in. But what had been a straightforward one-day story about the premier appearing on TV had turned into a week-long political cliffhanger. Will the government pay $50,000? Will the Liberals be part of the show? Will the Tories get all ten minutes? Will John Bassett spring for free air time? And so the story continued for almost a week, making it a high-profile event that viewers felt compelled to watch if only out of curiosity. The state of the provincial economy was of secondary interest.

Jim Bradley, the Liberal interim leader, spoke for the Grits. He was predictably less than riveting and his six minutes had little impact. The Tories had only the last four minutes of the show, and they used them to maximum effect. Mike Harris appeared with a brief message. He said, "The premier has just told you about the very serious state the province is in financially. The economic situation is very difficult and he is looking for your advice. I have a book here that has a series of options. We call it New Directions, Volume 1. If you would like your copy, call 1-800-668-MIKE."

Within twenty-four hours of that broadcast, the Tories received 14,000 phone calls and 5,000 faxes or letters asking for a copy of the New Directions series. They distributed 20,000 booklets on the basis of one four-minute time slot twenty-six minutes into the show.

"In order to be able to do that, you had to have a product. You had to understand that people want to dialogue – not to be lectured to. You have to have been 'on' the psychology of where people were at, to be able to catch the wave and understand it," said Lindsay. "All of the town hall meetings, all of the things we had done were captured in that four minutes. And 20,000 people asked for a copy of that booklet. When they said the Common Sense Revolution was a crazy, new unusual thing to do, people weren't paying attention to us – we'd done it several years before."

And they continued to do it, releasing booklets on crime and education and getting them out to anyone who asked for a copy. The New Directions series was the precursor; it set the stage for the Common Sense Revolution.

By January 1994, with the party debt coming under control, the Tories decided that it was time to start organizing for the upcoming election. That was when they appointed Tom Long and Leslie Noble as campaign co-chairs. Noble was no surprise. She was seen as a consensus builder, someone who could hold the campaign together. Long, however, was a gamble. While there was no question that he was capable and a hard worker, he had run afoul of some of the old guard, and it remained to be seen how he would fit in with the new team.

As it turned out, he was an inspired choice. Long was not just a brilliant strategist. He protected the party at media conferences and could field questions from a roomful of hostile media and not bat an eyelid. He also had a clear track record on the right of the party. He came to the Common Sense Revolution from conviction, rather than convenience. He was one of the first to enunciate a strong right-wing platform for the Tories. No one could accuse Long of trying to out-Reform Reform. Since his earliest days as president of the campus Tories, he had espoused a right-wing agenda. And, like every other member of the Tory team, he was absolutely dedicated to, and believed in, Mike Harris.

And so Lindsay, Long, and Noble buckled down to the tasks at hand. They became known as the triumvirate. Despite their disparate backgrounds, despite the fact that they had all worked for different and at times warring factions within the party, they discovered that they could work together very well. Collegiality was their code word. Everyone genuinely liked and respected one another.

"My inclination is always to be pretty headstrong and go ahead and do things on my own," Long said. "I had to learn to play with the other kids." So the campaign got under way.

They decided that one thing was fundamental. Decisions had to be made jointly. Long, Noble, and Lindsay started meeting at the King Edward Hotel in Toronto every Friday beginning in January 1994. They brainstormed on issues, on strategy, on who would do what in any campaign. They knew that what they were talking about was what the people of Ontario were talking about. But how could they get their message out to the people? How could they attract attention to what they were saying?

The challenge was to define themselves. They grew in number, moved from the King Edward, and developed into what came to be known as the Bradgate Group, named after the Bradgate Arms Hotel, which was their new meeting place. Gradually they brought more people into the group. Mitch Patten, who later became campaign secretary, was an obvious candidate for the inner circle. Alister Campbell, an insurance executive who later became their policy guru, was another natural. Jerry Redmond, the tsar of the Tory research section, and John Mykytyshyn, the Tory pollster, also came on board. Mykytyshyn had been with Mike Harris since 1990 and had worked on the Victoria-Haliburton by-election. Bill Young, chief executive officer of Consumers Distributing, and Tom Campbell, former Hydro chairman, who are friends of Tom Long, became members. Campbell brought an elder statesman-like presence to the table. George Boddington, who had been part of the long-range planning group, was included, and Tony Clement dropped in from time to time. As the campaign progressed, others came aboard. Paul Rhodes joined in January 1995, and he was followed by many more people once the election writ was dropped on 28 April.

Team-building and "bonding" one weekend at the Bradgate, they divided into groups of Liberals and Conservatives. Those who were Liberals put themselves in the Grits' shoes and played "wargames" over possible Liberal election strategy.

"We concluded very early on that the Liberals would play a very conservative game," Long said. "To be honest, we never did come up with a decent strategy for the NDP. It was hard to imagine what to do for them," he recalled. With his mischievous sense of humor, he couldn't help adding, "We came out with a Bob Rae-centric strategy, which was basically fire your entire cabinet, eliminate your party name, and run on a few key issues."

The Bradgate Group agreed that the Tories had to go big. They had to get out and make a big splash – before the election. The Tories knew that as soon as the election came along, everyone was going to be saying the same thing. They knew in their hearts that they had their own unique message, their own program, and their own platform, and they didn't want anyone to steal anything from them during the election.

In May 1994, they launched the Common Sense Revolution, a bold statement of their ideas on everything from welfare fraud to education. It was wildly successful. Lindsay said that once they had launched the CSR, it became clear that their gamble was going to pay off.

"Nobody was able to puncture holes in it," Lindsay recalled. "The attacks were all pejorative – Mike is a crazy man, this program is silly, it's flag-waving cheap tricks. We said, 'Look, do you want to debate the issues or do you want to talk about the color of the curtains?'"

Once they realized that the critics weren't attacking the substance of their platform, the Tories knew that they were on the right track. All they had to do was stick to their plan. And that's exactly what they did.

More importantly, that's what Mike Harris did. Harris had been closely involved with the drafting of the CSR, especially the section on workfare. He had intimate knowledge of the details. Unlike some party leaders, who have to be groomed and primed and briefed by advisers on the party platform, Harris knew exactly what the party platform was because he'd written parts of it himself. He knew it and he believed in it.

"He didn't have to memorize the book. He didn't have to study and learn the substance because he had been talking that way for two years. He had been listening to people. It wasn't as though we were saying here's a package, go try it and market this one. It was coming from within," Lindsay said.

The Bradgate Group helped with the strategic placement of the policy. The content of the Common Sense Revolution wasn't new or strange-looking to Mike Harris. What was new was the method by which it was launched. By July 1994, when no one had blasted the Common Sense Revolution out of the water, the Tories realized that all they had to do was wait – until the people started paying attention.

Chapter Nine

Sex, Half-truths, and Videotape

As the everlasting post-mortem dragged on and on about what went wrong with the Liberal campaign of 1995, three issues kept emerging. The first was gender. How much impact did the fact that the Liberal leader was a woman have on the campaign? The second was credibility, which had ramifications for all politicians. One of the major questions for voters was whom to believe. Were voters electing someone they trusted or someone they believed was lying the least? The third was videotapes. In the last week of the campaign, the Tories targeted sixty-six ridings with videotapes outlining their policies and introducing their local candidate. The Grits should have known they'd do it, since videos had been highly successful for the Tories in the Victoria-Haliburton by-election. So why didn't the Liberals use the same technique to target what every poll told them was a high number of undecided voters?

The question of gender is a perplexing one. Did McLeod lose because she's a woman? Or did she lose because she was perceived as being indecisive. Was she perceived as being indecisive because that's how women are often seen? Or was she seen as indecisive because she *was* indecisive? Are voters in Ontario still so unsophisticated that they don't want to see a woman as premier?

Yes, said some Liberals, in the wake of the defeat. Some will cite anecdotal evidence of hostility at the door, with people making sexist comments about the Liberal leader's gender. Even so, even the most ardent Grit has to admit that if gender were an issue, it was never a deciding factor. And pollster Conrad Winn has some interesting insights on the role of gender in the campaign. It can play both ways, commented Winn, chairman of the Ottawa-based COMPAS polling.

"It probably helped Lyn McLeod get the leadership, given her checkered career as a minister. The fact that women were fashionable, at the time that she was a candidate, may perhaps have accounted for the increment that made her the leader."

Moreover, Winn said that gender may have been important in areas that are difficult to detect on the telephone.

"One of the things that has happened to women is that women, ironically and paradoxically, have a confidence to criticize women and to criticize feminists because women today have freedoms that they didn't have thirty years ago," he continued. "And one of the paradoxes is that women quite often sympathize with what they perceive to be male victims of excessively aggressive women. And in the leadership debate some women would have been turned off by McLeod, whom they perceived as taking advantage of her being a woman to interrupt with impunity her male contenders. Clearly there would be women who would relish the idea of a woman premier. 'About time,' they might feel. But it can play both ways."

Grit pollster Michael Marzolini crunched numbers to show that while there was a significant gender gap in party support, with women more likely to have voted Liberal and men more likely to have voted Tory, it ironically played little part in this election. This gap was traditional and historic and had nothing to do with the gender of each party's leader. Marzolini's company, Insight Canada Research, produced polling results that showed a substantial bias among Ontario voters which favors male candidates for premier. Specifically, one in five (21 percent) Ontarians believed that there were more advantages to having a man as premier, while only 8 percent felt that it was better to have a woman leader. Male and female voters shared this same belief in almost equal numbers.

In a post-election analysis, Marzolini said that this view had very little impact on the 1995 election, since one-half (50 percent) of those who felt that there were more advantages to having a man as premier voted PC this election, compared to 46 percent of all respondents, making the gender gap count for as little as four percentage points. One-third (32 percent) of those who felt that there were more advantages to having a woman as premier voted Liberal, compared to 29 percent of other voters.

The main advantage associated with male leadership was the perception that men are more tough and decisive, and that they are more respected and taken more seriously.

"It was only a very small factor," said Marzolini, but it nevertheless influenced people's votes.

"I don't think that's going to be that much of a factor – though it had an influence, a lot of things had an influence. If your neighbor has a sign on his or her lawn, that's an influence. It had only a small influence on people's votes. This shows that 4 percent of people were influenced to vote PC because of gender. It had a small direct influence on the actual election outcome."

McLeod's gender by itself was not a significant factor. It was on the menu along with a number of items that affected the outcome of the election. According to Marzolini's post-election report, other issues were more significant. On a scale of one to ten, with ten being very influential and one being not at all influential, five items topped the poll.

First (at 7.85), the PCs were the only alternative to the NDP to spell out policies clearly. Second (at 7.67), people felt that Harris would do a better job than McLeod. Third (at 7.33), there was the idea that it was time to give the PCs a chance. Fourth (at 7.26), people felt that the PCs held many of their own values. And fifth (at 7.18), there was the feeling that Ontario needed radical or revolutionary change.

So if it wasn't gender, perhaps it was the credibility of the candidate herself that caused the abrupt turnaround in Liberal fortunes. It soon became apparent in the campaign that it wasn't only gay and lesbian demonstrators who wanted McLeod to come out of the closet with her policies. Who really knew what she stood for?

Her handlers, and they were legion, didn't help matters. They created a bubble around their candidate, a plastic facade that was impossible for reporters to break through. They forced the public to play peek-a-boo with their candidate, controlling her, managing her, and, most of all, keeping her at a safe distance. Chief among those who tried to control media access to McLeod was Jim McLean, who became notorious for his "two more questions, please" line, which he threw into scrums and press conferences any time his leader got into hot water. The Liberal campaign was so carefully orchestrated that McLeod was never in a position to be confronted by the great unwashed. Unfortunately, the great unwashed rarely vote for a leader whom they have never met. The strategy backfired badly.

It seemed as if the Grit plan was to let her ride Prime Minister Jean Chrétien's coattails to victory. It was such a transparent ploy that wags on the campaign trail dubbed McLeod "Chrétien in drag."

But the Grits were sitting with what they perceived to be a two-to-one lead in the polls. Why bother getting her out to the electorate when they were doing so well keeping her under wraps? It may have been one of the biggest mistakes of the Liberal campaign. Few people in the province knew or recognized Lyn McLeod, the rookie leader. Most people couldn't even remember her name.

People needed to get to know her, to find out where she was coming from – not because they wanted to trash her or trip her up, but because voters have a natural curiosity about the people whom they are about to elect. And McLeod's handlers did nothing to satisfy that curiosity.

The Tories, on the other hand, took big chances bringing their leader to the people as much as possible and putting him in some high-risk situations in order to get their message across to the voters. Their policy announcement on employment equity, for example, took place in a Scarborough high school where most of the students were members of visible minorities.

The Liberal platform appeared to voters to be a pale imitation of the Tory one. If the Common Sense Revolution was Tory Blue, the Liberal platform was Blue Lite. When the Tories promised to cut taxes and balance the budget, the Liberals promised to cut taxes and balance the budget. If the New Democrats promised to keep post-secondary education affordable and build four subways, McLeod promised to keep post-secondary education affordable and build four subways. The Liberals ducked and weaved so much on policy, no one was quite sure where the next policy was coming from.

The great joy of being a Liberal in Ontario is that you can drift left for folk who like tax-and-spend policies or you can drift right for those who'd prefer a little slash and burn in their lives. In short, you can be all things to all people. In an election campaign, that is. Getting people to vote for those promises, in these days of the cynical electorate, was something else entirely.

Liberal flacks, however, were terrified of slipping up. Still smarting from the hostile publicity that dumped David Peterson in 1990, they were scared silly that some off-the-cuff remark by their leader would sink them this time around. So they shrink-wrapped her and kept her away from anything vaguely controversial. Even the launch of the puff-ball Red Book was staged in such a way as to exclude informed debate. Scores of reporters and photographers were jammed into a glitzy ballroom at the Four Seasons Hotel in Yorkville for the announcement. McLeod answered a handful of superficial questions before being whisked away by handlers. It was hardly a scintillating performance.

When the Tories announced a Sunday-morning press briefing to dissect figures in the Red Book, it wasn't Tory flacks who phoned reporters about it; it was the Grits. Liberals posted a spin doctor at the doorway of the building housing Tory headquarters to make sure media members were dutifully spun with the gospel according to the Grits.

Voters didn't believe Lyn McLeod and her 140-odd promises, because the figures didn't add up. How can you promise to build GO tracks to Kitchener and even dream of building four subway lines in Metro if you're serious about balancing the books?

Dubbed the "In-the-Red Book'" by critics, the Grit platform begged three questions:

What did Lyn McLeod and the Liberals learn from three-and-a-half years of David Peterson and his government? The answer was nothing.

What would they do differently if they were in power now? The answer was nothing.

And what would set a Liberal government apart from an NDP one? Again, the answer was nothing.

The New Democrats played into voter cynicism by promising nothing and then accusing McLeod of mixing up election day, 8 June, with Christmas. Of course, voters knew all about broken promises. They'd heard the sound of crashing NDP election pledges for five years. The electorate were tired of half-truths and half-baked policies. They wanted something concrete and substantial.

That left Mike Harris and the Tories. There was a broad constituency out there that desperately wanted the province to move to the right on fiscal matters, but these people didn't believe it would ever happen. The Tories knew that this was their biggest problem. It explains why they were so eager to get their candidate out to the people. And they dropped him into some fairly high-risk situations.

Announcing the end of employment equity in the heart of multicultural Scarborough, as Harris did, could have been disastrous. Yet it worked. His team had to make voters see that Harris was committed to this plan. And the blueprint for implementing this kind of radical departure already existed. Voters only had to look at Ralph Klein in Alberta or Frank McKenna in New Brunswick to see that Ontario could axe bureaucrats, tighten up on welfare, and slash taxes.

Ontario had a bigger deficit than all the other provinces combined. Alberta, Manitoba, Saskatchewan, New Brunswick, and Newfoundland all managed to get their financial houses in order. All have balanced budgets in 1995. New Brunswick and Newfoundland had the toughest battle because they ran out of fish, one of the mainstays of their provincial economies. And federal transfer payments, their second-largest source of income, were cut back substantially. Yet they still managed to get out of the red. Voters looked at the other provinces and realized that what Ontario needed was leadership. And that perception – not gender – is why they elected Mike Harris.

Then there were the videotapes. They were another oddity that received very little press, and yet they may have influenced the outcome of the campaign far more than sex and lies. Ironically, the videotape idea came partly from the Reform Party, which had used them in B.C. and in a couple of Ontario ridings. Tony Clement, who originally saw the potential of videos, asked the makers to do a presentation to the Tory team before the 1994 Victoria-Haliburton by-election, in which former Haliburton reeve Chris Hodgson was elected. Campaign co-chair Leslie Noble was an instant convert.

"We did a test market in the Victoria-Haliburton by-election," recalled Noble. "We had good discussions with people across Canada who'd used them before. There was some evidence of them being used before in the U.K. and in the States, and we were really interested in it because it seemed like a way of introducing a candidate to a constituent in the age of cocooning. You don't have to be invasive. You don't have to invade their home, their private lives. You can look at it the comfort of your own home without feeling threatened."

The videos were used in the last week of the Victoria-Haliburton by-election and proved highly effective in targeting undecided voters. Their success convinced the Tories to use them in sixty-six targeted ridings in the province-wide election.

The process of producing and distributing them was rather simple. Campaign headquarters helped candidates write their own scripts, made a bulk deal with a dubbing house, and negotiated a good per unit price. The videos cost two dollars each, which is one dollar less than it cost for a lawn sign, but the tapes imparted a lot more information than the usual "vote for so-and-so" sign message. The candidates paid for the videos themselves.

Tony Clement was one of those candidates. Running in Brampton South, he bought 4,000 seven-minute videos and distributed them during the final days of the campaign. Clement targeted every fifth house in some areas and every undecided voter whom he had encountered in his personal canvassing. There were instructions on the box to pass the video along to a neighbor or return it to his campaign office when they had finished with it. By the last day of the campaign, Clement found that he was canvassing streets where every house had seen the video. On election day, Clement defeated the incumbent Liberal Bob Callahan.

In the end, the Tories distributed 250,000 videos in their sixty-six targeted ridings, reaching an estimated one million voters. In a replay of the Victoria-Haliburton by-election, they were wildly successful. Why?

There was a master video with a standardized format, into which local candidates and their communities were dubbed. The videos enabled the Tories to distribute on a massive scale a standardized message about Mike Harris and the Common Sense Revolution. They provided what every campaign dreams of – a large number of candidates all saying the same thing on party policy.

Targeting the undecided was a central element in the video strategy. It worked in Victoria-Haliburton, and it worked in the provincial election. If you only have limited dollars to spend on a campaign, don't waste money on (a) people who are committed Tories or (b) people who are such die-hard Liberals or NDP that there's no way you could convince them to vote Conservative. To win the election, the Tories had to target the undecided. With that in mind, Noble set out to research the new voter volatility that had become such a significant factor in recent elections in Ontario.

"There's no party loyalty – or very little compared to ten years ago, and you've seen it in the massive voter shifts," Noble said. "If you examine the results of the 1993 federal election and the 1990 provincial election, you see massive shifts first to the NDP and then to the Reform Party.

"Ideologically, that doesn't make sense, and yet the shifts are happening in many of the same areas." Traditional swing ridings, where people moved back and forth between Liberal and PC, where a 5 percent swing meant the difference between winning or losing a riding, are no longer the norm.

The Tories conducted a huge analysis of the past two provincial elections and the 1993 federal election and came up with a formula for how voting had changed in Ontario. They ranked ridings based on the volatility index.

"If you just looked at sheer volatility, ridings like Peterborough-

Hastings, Victoria-Haliburton, all of those were at the top," said Noble. "We first did that analysis at the end of the Victoria-Haliburton by-election, and without any coaching from us it spit out Victoria-Haliburton as one of the most volatile." They then selected those ridings where they had no sitting members and therefore no on-the-ground institutional strength. Next they took ridings where there was a high volatility factor. They were researched thoroughly, and the constituents were sent direct mail on the top issues of the day. It was these ridings that were targeted for videos.

"The videos played a big role in that when people were ready to make up their minds and decide if they actually could trust the people they were voting for, I think it made a big difference, because they actually got to see a little bit more about their candidate than they might otherwise have done.

"You see Mike Harris on the news every day, but you don't always know a lot about your local Harris candidate," Noble said.

The question is, why didn't the Liberals go with their own tapes? In fact, Liberal campaign manager Bob Richardson considered using videos but decided against it.

"We looked at it, we even did some research on it, and we decided we didn't think it was as effective as other people did. That may in fact have been an error," Richardson said.

"It's costly, which was one of the things we had a problem with in terms of doing it. It would certainly be costly on the scale they did it," he said.

Chapter Ten

Mussel Power

R umor has it that the idea for the Common Sense Revolution
was hatched in the winter of 1993-94 over bottles of wine
and bowls of mussels at a small restaurant called Episode, a
few blocks from Maple Leaf Gardens. After day-long strategy sessions, Leslie Noble, Tom Long, Alister Campbell, David Lindsay,
Mitch Patten, and an assortment of other people would retire,
exhausted, to a simple communal meal of mussels. They'd shuck the
shells, stir the mussels into the tomato sauce, and then take turns
dipping hunks of bread into the sauce. As they ate, they continued
to discuss strategy, analyze policy, and map out the road to the election. In many ways, these meals were symbolic of how the upcoming campaign would be conducted. It was teamwork, everyone getting together and sharing their ideas, opinions, and suggestions.

The Victoria-Haliburton by-election was one of the major
milestones on the road to the general election. The Liberals were
ahead by 20 points in the opinion polls ten days before the by-election vote, but the Tories countered by bringing in their seven-
minute videos aimed at swaying the large undecided vote. In the
end Chris Hodgson was elected with more than 50 percent of the
popular vote. It was a stunning victory, giving the new, young Tory
team a much needed boost.

Tory insiders said that Lyn McLeod and the Liberals totally
misread the result of the March 1994 vote, and some of those same
insiders claimed that it was the main cause of the Liberal downfall
in 1995. Liberals believed they had lost because of McLeod's stand

on same-sex spousal benefits. McLeod and the Liberals were supporting legislation to give gay and lesbian partners spousal benefits.
During the by-election campaign, the Tories simply repeated their
policy on spousal benefits – that it wasn't an issue. Jobs and the
economy were the main issues. That was the message which they
had heard from their town hall meetings. Gay rights might have
been a topic dear to the heart of a vocal minority in downtown
Toronto, but it didn't tip the scales in rural Muskoka.

The Tories did a poll in the wake of the by-election and discovered that the videos had won it for them. But the Liberals remained
convinced that the same-sex issue cost them the riding. The Liberal
analysis soon became conventional wisdom for the media pundits.
McLeod's initial stand on same-sex benefits triggered a pressure
within the Liberal Party that forced her to back off from her original position. The official Liberal line was that the party could not
support same-sex spousal benefits because of the adoption clause
that was introduced into the legislation.

It was a cynical flip-flop. Grit strategists saw what they perceived to be the writing on the wall – that same-sex issues didn't
play well in rural Ontario – and changed their policy to fit what
was perceived to be the message. In fact, instead of looking at the
graffiti, they should have been watching the videos – because the
videos had won it for the Tories.

Misreading the by-election results so badly was a huge mistake
on the part of the Liberals. It was an early indication of how much
they were willing to change policy according to political circumstances. But people were looking for some consistency – and fairness – in the political opinions of their party leaders. McLeod paid
a massive price for her flip-flop. She was just too willing to bend
with the wind.

In the wake of the by-election, Long, Noble, and Campbell
held a number of strategy meetings. They knew that Mike Harris
wanted to get a platform out early, and that he wanted to go big.
However, they had a brand label problem. The words "Progressive"
and "Conservative" caused a meltdown in the minds of most
Ontarians. There were even some within the party who wanted to
dump the name completely. The old label would have to go.

On the more positive side, the policy gurus knew that Harris continued to be more popular than the other two leaders, although he wasn't very well known. The Tories were on to a good thing when they compared Harris to McLeod, a relative unknown, and to Bob Rae, who was known all too well. Harris was the best thing the Tories had going for them.

And voters wanted change – major change. It was urgently needed, but they did not believe that any politician would deliver it. They just didn't believe that any elected official would do what they said they were going to do. But while there was a withering cynicism out there, there was also a nascent hope, a belief in democracy, a belief that the system still worked.

Harris, at his town hall meetings, became a lightning rod for all that cynicism. It was a revelation. Jobs were the number one issue, a huge reversal in fat cat Ontario where everyone was used to virtually full employment.

So the Common Sense Revolution was born. The name itself was controversial at first. There were some who thought that the revolution part pushed things a little too far. But Harris liked the Common Sense part of it, and many Tories liked the oxymoron ring to the name. If you're not going to run under Progressive Conservative, which is also an oxymoron, then why not have some fun and go from one oxymoron to another? The name Common Sense Revolution wasn't road-tested in focus groups or in any other formal way. The financially beleaguered Tories didn't have the money at the time. But the name had a resonance, it projected an image which they were trying to get across, and it captured the imaginations of party members. In true Tom Long fashion, it took only five weeks to launch the Common Sense Revolution.

It was, said Campbell, "one of the most exciting things I have ever been involved with in my life." The Tories worked like crazy. Mike Harris told them what he wanted in the plan. Jobs, he said, were the number one priority. And taxes had to come down to stimulate the economy. And then, he said, he wanted to get the deficit under control. Jobs were difficult. A tax cut would be a tall order – that would mean more budget cuts. And they had to respect the electorate – you can't take these people and trick them.

"This plan has to be real," Harris told his strategists.

That's where Midland Walwyn financial wizard Mark Mullins came into the picture. Mullins had phoned Tony Clement in Mike Harris's office, out of the blue, to offer his help on the campaign. He became the Tories' key financial strategist. He made sure that the numbers added up. In the year preceding the election, he would walk a variety of commentators and journalists through the plan and show them just how the numbers worked. He was the Tories' main number cruncher, providing endless models of how to balance this if you take away that.

"In the end," said Campbell, "it wasn't all that hard to write the policy because we had so much to draw from." And he added that Harris's hand was in the plan every step of the way. It was not a plan they drew up and handed over to their leader. It was the leader who insisted that the plan be put into writing. The CSR underwent fourteen drafts, and changes to the last three drafts were made in Harris's handwriting. In fact, the CSR was the product of a great many hands. Campbell drove the process for a while, David Lindsay followed him, and then Deb Hutton, a policy strategist in Harris's office, took up where Lindsay left off. Close Harris aide Bill King worked on yet another draft. In the end, Harris and Glen Stone directed the writing and rewriting.

As well, the Tories had a brilliant research team at Queen's Park, led by Jerry Redmond. They, too, had an immense amount of input into the plan. Bill Young, CEO of Consumer's Distributing, contributed three weeks of work, and Mark Mullins ran each new version through his model and sent them back for revisions. The team provided a number of draft options, and Harris chose the final one.

This represented a radical change in backroom politics. The CSR wasn't formulated by a bunch of cigar-chomping strategists writing high-blown election rhetoric in smoke-filled committee rooms. This was a group of people who came up with workable solutions, and their leader was not just window-dressing; he was an intrinsic part of the process.

Then the Tories began the long, slow task of rebuilding the party's credibility, essential to the success of the 1995 campaign.

While the CSR didn't pay any big dividends by way of poll numbers immediately after it was announced, it did pay off big time in attracting candidates. If people were going to put their careers on the line, they had to have a pretty good reason to do so. Campbell estimates that more than half the candidates who put their names forward did so because of the CSR, and because Harris had the intestinal fortitude to bring the CSR out early. Donations started to improve, not necessarily from corporations, but from individuals who saw the plan, liked it, and threw in their five, ten or fifteen dollars. The amounts were small but invaluable.

The Tories experienced a tough period between the time they planted the seed of the CSR and when it finally bloomed. The campaign team told their candidates that the poll numbers wouldn't move until the last two weeks of the election campaign. They told them to sit tight and not to budge. They told them not to panic. But it was a hard sell. All through the fall of 1994 and the spring of 1995, the Liberals sat with a two-to-one edge in the polls, and some Tories started to wonder if those numbers would ever change in their favor. The only people who didn't blink were Harris and the campaign team. No matter what happened, no matter how bad things seemed, they didn't change their tune.

In the meantime, the Tories were out recruiting candidates. And it was a very unusual candidate search. They weren't going to allow themselves to be suckered into running the same old party hacks who run in every election. "It was the most thorough and open process that our party had ever undertaken," recalled Tony Clement. First off, there were no promises. No one was lured to run for the Tories with promises of a cabinet position. It just wasn't done, and Harris insisted that it had to be that way. And they wouldn't guarantee nominations. Clement received calls from several prospective candidates asking how to get a nomination. "Sell more memberships than the other people and make sure they come out on nomination night, and that's how you win" was Clement's answer. It was in direct contrast to the Liberal nomination process. They flipped the Rolodex and came up with a bunch of old names from the David Peterson era. Clement pointed out that getting a nomination takes political skill and savvy, the same kind of skill and savvy that parachuted candidates, for instance, may not have.

The Tories started their candidate search at the beginning of 1992. By the end of the following year, they had 600 names of would-be candidates on a database. They developed rules about nominations. For example, ridings had to have a minimum number of members signed up before they could hold a nomination meeting, and the number of members had to equal 5 percent of the Tory popular vote in the last election or 500, whichever was less. If the Tory candidate in the last election got 9,000 votes, the riding association had to have at least 450 members signed up before they could hold a nomination meeting. This rule stopped the traditional Tory habit of running the riding president, who may have run two or three times before, and brought in fresh blood. It also forced the riding associations to satisfy headquarters that they had done an adequate candidate search.

When the nomination process was complete, the papers had to be signed off by Clement, the party executive, the campaign team, and finally Harris himself.

It was an exhaustive system, but it ensured that the candidate search in each riding was broad and open and the best one possible. The Tories attracted a lot of new faces. Only one former MP and former MPP won nominations. Environment minister Brenda Elliott is the product of the new system. She ran against the riding president in Guelph, but had the party used its old system, it's doubtful that she could have won. Ridings that didn't follow the rules were hauled onto the carpet and told to start the nomination process over.

Once a candidate was nominated, he or she was sent to candidate school. It was tough. There was a test. You had to pay attention. David Lindsay gave an introductory speech on how Mike Harris had got them to the point where they were at. And then Leslie Noble walked the candidates through endless slides with polling numbers. Good news and bad news. Here's what we have to move, here's how we're going to do it, and this is what's going to happen. And then Alister Campbell took candidates line by line through the CSR. Finally, there was an exam, which Campbell marked and handed back to candidates at the end of the session. It was a very telling exercise. Some candidates hadn't looked at the material at all, figuring it was just another brochure to be stuffed in a mailbox. One candidate, who is now a member of cabinet, actually failed and was devastated. It wasn't until the policy training session that he realized that the party was serious about this stuff and that he needed to get his act together if he was going to make the grade. A few days after the exam, Campbell got a call from the candidate, telling him to ask him anything about the plan. This time, the guy had it all down pat. "I'm not a failing kind of guy," he told Campbell.

It was a bold strategy, but it got everyone singing from the same policy hymn book, and when was the last time, Tory insiders mused, when all the Tories were spouting the same policies at the same time in an election campaign?

During the winter of 1995, strategists guided the candidates through the model of the Tory campaign. They would hammer home their message in the first two weeks of the campaign, and the Liberals would put out a big, fat red book. Then the Tories would start making progress before the debate, but probably no poll would come out before then. Numbers would close rapidly after the debate – not because of the debate, but because of stuff that had already been happening before, but people would credit the debate. Then it would become a huge race between Harris and McLeod, and the Tories would win. They would pull ahead with ten days to go. And the Liberals would start to go negative on Mike, and it would not work. That was how the Tories saw the campaign unfolding as early as November 1994.

The Liberal campaign was predictable. Five months before the election, after a brainstorming session of the Bradgate Group, the Tories told their candidates that the Liberals would come out with the Red Book on the Thursday of the first full week of the campaign. Sure enough, they were right. The Liberals just kept doing exactly what the Tories expected a front-runner to do. They ran a replica of the Chrétien campaign.

The Red Book, from front to back cover, was bogged down in double-talk. In the first two weeks of the campaign the Liberals didn't talk about a balanced budget or welfare reform. In the week before the debate, the polling gap had closed by half, dropping from 26 to 13 points, the result of a week-long attack on corporate handouts and welfare fraud and outlining Harris's workfare plan. The Tories had anticipated eight of those points. They called it the "air pocket." Once people discovered who McLeod was, the numbers would drop even more. After the election, the campaign team heard one sentence over and over from Tory candidates, "It happened just the way you said it would."

What also worked well was the careful balance between Tom Long and Leslie Noble. Noble had a genius for team-building. She had a flair for organization. Long gracefully accepted her talents for organization and found that anytime he needed to get something done, Noble was there to arrange it. As well, the Tories took a radical approach to polling. Where other parties relied on one pollster to provide polling and analysis, their pollster, John Mykytyshyn of Canadian Voter Contact, sat down with the campaign team, and together they analyzed the data. Mykytyshyn realized that the entire team had been involved in numerous campaigns and that they were all experienced at interpreting poll data.

According to the Tories, Mykytyshyn was an incredibly accurate pollster. He was one of the few pollsters to predict that David Peterson would lose his seat in 1990. Nobody believed him. He was spot-on in Harris's leadership campaign. He called every by-election correctly, and he called the Tory numbers to within 0.2 percent on election night.

In the end, it was the consistency of the year-long Tory campaign that paid the biggest dividends. Their leader was true to his principles. He didn't rewrite the party platform on the fly. With the exception of a couple of slips, one on university tenure and one on the Windsor casino, Harris was focused and credible. He believed in his campaign. So too did the riding offices. They eagerly bought into the Common Sense Revolution. You could visit any Tory campaign office in any riding in Ontario and find the same message, the same set of firmly held beliefs. The Tories quietly dropped the Progressive Conservative moniker and changed their party color from traditional blue to a new Tory purple. The team dubbed it "revolutionary blue," even though it looked purple to some people.

Regardless, the new shade racked up points with focus groups.

The new revolutionary-blue campaign signs sporting the message "Common sense ... for a change" were clearly identifiable across the province. The same picture of Mike Harris decorated every campaign office. All Tory candidates were handing out the same literature on the Common Sense Revolution – tax cuts for jobs, work for welfare, scrap the quota law.

Victory was the pay-off for getting the message out early. It was the pay-off for picking a group of people who got along and believed in Mike Harris. While the Liberal campaign was built along a traditional brokerage model of picking candidates from the left and the right and balancing the team with women, the Tories asked only one question: Do you believe in Mike?

Chapter Eleven

Hey, Presto! Reform Vanishes

As the grey dawn broke, on 26 October 1993, the day after the federal election, shocked Ontario Tories took a look at the headlines and started to hyperventilate. Politically, that is. The Grits had swept the province, taking 98 out of 99 seats. Simcoe Centre was the only seat that they didn't win. It went to Ed Harper, the first Reformer elected in Ontario.

It wasn't the Liberal tide that worried the Tories. Far from it. They figured that a couple of years and half-a-dozen broken Red Book promises later, Ontario would be ready to embrace small "c" conservatism. No, what bothered them was the remarkable showing by the Reform Party. Reform had obliterated the Tories in Western Canada, and while they had made only one successful raid into Ontario, the signs of a strong Reform presence were clearly there for anyone to see. Ontario's Tories knew they had to deal with Reform, and somehow convince Preston Manning and his party not to make a foray into provincial politics in the upcoming provincial election.

In their research on the 1990 election, the Tories discovered that the presence of fourth parties meant a difference between a minority and a majority government for the NDP. If the Tories had picked up two-thirds of the fourth-party vote that went to groups such as the Family Coalition Party, they would have won 10 extra seats in the legislature. Instead of only 20 seats, they would have had a far more respectable 30, leaving the NDP to form a minority government.

It fell to former party president and newly elected Brampton South MPP Tony Clement to staunch the flow of votes from the Conservatives to fourth parties. The biggest fourth-party headache for the Tories was the threat of Reform running in Ontario. The federal Tories obviously had failed to respect Reform. Ontario Tories didn't want to make the same colossal blunder. Clement, son of former Ontario attorney general John Clement, gave himself the task of learning everything about the western-based party that had wreaked such havoc with his federal counterparts.

"I wanted to learn not only about them, but to allow them to learn about us," Clement recalled. "We were absolutely convinced that if they were to look at us, and look at where we were coming from, we might not be able to satisfy them on 100 percent of the stuff, but we could satisfy them on 80 percent of it. And maybe that would be enough to reduce or eliminate the threat of splitting the vote and allowing 130 Liberals to get in, just as we'd seen 98 out of 99 Liberals federally in the province of Ontario."

The Tories took a two-pronged approach. They planned to make connections with the grass roots as well as the elite of the Reform Party. Concerning the grass roots, Clement hit pay dirt when he acquired a fairly comprehensive list of every Reform member in Ontario, some 25,000 names. The Tories sent out mailings incessantly to every Reform member on that list, with letters that went a little like this.

"Hi, my name's Mike Harris. You don't know a lot about me but here's some policy. Here's where we stand as a provincial party. You might be interested in it."

The plan was always to lead with policy. Grass-roots people talk about policy. There was no point telling people to vote Conservative to avoid splitting the vote. Voters have no stake in strategic voting. They simply don't care. Main Street Ontarians care deeply about issues. Reformers hate the old top-down style of politics and like discussions on policy. The Tories caught the wave. In mailing after mailing, they asked the Reformers for their opinions – on education, crime, and the deficit. They sent out questionnaires and were amazed at the number that were returned.

So the Tories wrote back to the Reformers, thanking them for their answers and sending them even more policy statements and asking their opinions yet again. They treated these Reform members with tender loving care throughout this process, which took a year and a half. Their aim was to make the grass roots of the Reform Party familiar with Mike Harris and feel comfortable with his policies.

"We were very, very clear though, in our dealings with them that we weren't going to change who we were for them. Mike was very clear on this. We would share information with them. We should share who we were. If they felt comfortable with us, that was their choice, come on board. We're an open party. You can join up, you can get involved in the riding associations, etc.

"If you do not feel comfortable with us, this is who we are, we are not going to change who we are for you, but we understand," Clement said. He stressed that there was never any intention to "out reform Reform."

"We never said, 'How can we change ourselves to make ourselves more acceptable to you?'" Clement recalled. That would have been as much an affront to Reform followers as it would have been to mainstream Conservatives. The Tories kept it simple: they shared policy statements, introduced their leader Mike Harris, and told Reformers that they were welcome to climb aboard.

A lot of Reform members took up the invitation and easily integrated themselves with the Tories at the riding level. In Cambridge, the federal Reform Party candidate headed up the candidate search committee for the Tories' provincial candidate. In Durham West and in Al Palladini's riding of York Centre, Reformers were members of the executive.

In addition to courting grass-roots Reformers, the Ontario Tories set out to create a working relationship with the movers and shakers within the federal Reform Party. Mike Harris met three times with Reform Party leader Preston Manning, the first meeting taking place in December 1993. They met again on 3 May 1994. At that time, Harris and Clement talked to Manning, his campaign manager Rick Anderson, and Ed Harper, the only Reformer from Ontario, prior to the release of the Common Sense Revolution. They shared with Manning and his people their ideas on welfare reform, tax cuts, and deficit reduction, and they asked the Reformers if they had any ideas which they wanted to share with them. The provincial Tories needed Manning and Reform on side. More specifically, they needed to spell out to Manning that there was no room on the right for a fourth party in the Ontario election. (Before the Tories left Ottawa, they discussed their radical plan with Tory leader Jean Charest, his policy gurus, and Conservative senators.)

The third phase of the campaign to deal with the Reform threat took place the day after the launch of the Common Sense Revolution in the spring of 1994. Harris met with Manning and his people and then the Tory caucus. They invited Jean Chrétien and the Liberals, but they were too busy. Ah, well.

Essentially, said Clement, they were treating the federal Reform Party with respect, while not trying to pretend to be something they were not. As a result, Manning decided not to branch into provincial politics. In October 1994, Tory efforts paid off. In an official vote at the Reform General Assembly, close to 70 percent of the members from Ontario and two-thirds of the Canada-wide membership voted against running candidates in provincial elections.

Clement attributed the higher vote in Ontario to the massive effort which the Tories had made to get their message out to Reform members in that province. There were no deals struck, no high-powered strategic discussions. It was a matter of each leader setting out policy and forging informal links. Formal ties were far less important than getting to know each other.

And it worked. Reform stayed home during the 1995 election.

Chapter Twelve

This Bus Was a Gas

I was five minutes late for the Liberal bus one morning. It pulled out of Queen's Park as my cab arrived. Taking a look at that day's *Toronto Sun*, I knew why the Grit wagonmaster had left me behind. Peter Worthington ruminated on why Lyn McLeod was losing this election campaign, Lorrie Goldstein handed out gratuitous advice to Mike Harris on how to win, and I decried the Grits' tacky politics of desperation. As one reporter pointed out to me, I should have been grateful that the bus didn't run me over as it roared away.

Faced with an otherwise empty day, I turned to the Tories. The Tory bus never left reporters behind. Well, except for once in North Bay, and as soon as they realized what they'd done, they dispatched a bus to pick up the straggler. But the Liberals didn't send a van to pick me up. Oh, no. The Grits were quite anal-retentive about timing. They had left several reporters behind before me. About the only thing the Liberals weren't wishy-washy about in this campaign was the time their bus left Queen's Park.

As it was, I was deeply crushed to miss their trip to Hamilton and Etobicoke. And you can't help wondering why those Grit politicians, who wring their hands about welfare moms, couldn't have spared a thought for a working mom who had to get her kids to school and make the bus by 7:45. How mean-spirited of them.

But never mind. The Tories understood. They had toasted bagels and hot coffee and words of sympathy. Everything on the bus anyone could need. I suspected that the Tories could rustle up a gin and tonic in an emergency, although here in sober NDP Ontario there's probably a law against gin on buses.

I am quite certain that here in the province of equal opportunity the NDP bus never would have left me standing by the curb. Regardless of my politics, or whatever nasty things I may have said about Premier Bob Rae, I am confident that the socialist shepherd herding reporters onto their bus would have remembered their government's "numerical targets." These were not quotas. No, Rae wouldn't call them that. But I am sure that the NDP is mindful of their legislation that could whack my employer, the *Toronto Sun*, with a hefty fine if it didn't hire its fair share of women. The NDP bus would wait for me until hell froze over, or the Liberals returned to power, whichever came first – if only to maintain a politically correct quota of women on the tour bus.

But campaigns on the bus aren't what they used to be. While there are still the obligatory hikes up to Kapuskasing, Thunder Bay, and Sudbury, reporters are usually flown there, rather than driven. There are no long swings through the wilds of Ontario with rum-swilling reporters – male, of course – carousing until the wee hours and occasionally whipping off the odd story to placate the editors back home. Fewer news outlets sent reporters on the buses full time in 1995. Radio station CFRB, which has the largest radio audience in the country, chose not to send its Queen's Park reporter Hal Vincent full time on the buses. He concentrated on Metro and vicinity.

"There were very few days when there wasn't at least one of the leaders in Toronto ... sometimes two and one day all three. The media are so concentrated in Toronto. What they tended to do was make a major announcement in Toronto and then hit the road, so that all the major radio stations, TV outlets and newspapers would be able to get to the main announcement," said Vincent.

The last recession and soaring costs are largely responsible for the media outlets reducing their bus coverage. It cost them a basic $18,000 to cover all three buses full time during the last election. As well, new expensive television satellite trucks have revolutionized coverage of the election, since they can transmit live from just about any point in the province.

So much for sweaty, ink-stained scribes scribbling furiously in the back of the bus. These days, we're still sweaty, but the average reporter also has to have an advanced grasp of fairly complex computer technology and be able to juggle a cell phone, fax machines, and all manner of new information technology – all without spilling your drink.

But the buses are still the first barometer of any campaign. Since the mood of the campaign tends to spill over onto the media bus, reporters on the victor's bus usually have a merrier time.

"Buses can be a dreary place at times," said Vincent, who was on the Grossman bus when his campaign was going down the tubes. "That kind of had a funereal atmosphere to it, especially towards the end."

The 1990 Liberal campaign produced a similar experience. Vincent remarked that the media had no inkling that David Peterson and the Grits were in trouble in the polls until, quite out of the blue, Peterson announced a 1 percent cut in the provincial sales tax, a policy that was at odds with that of Peterson's own finance minister, Bob Nixon.

Vincent was on Bob Rae's bus and asked him about the sales tax cut. "Aha," replied Rae, "we've got them on the run."

The Tory bus was the party wagon in the 1995 election. It's bold decals featuring pictures of Harris and blow-ups of news stories about the Common Sense Revolution were the brainchild of Lynne Atkinson. She was also responsible for the "Harry Rosen" photo of the Tory leader. It set a more casual tone for the campaign. The bus turned heads at every stop, and drivers pulled alongside, craning to read the news stories.

The interior was largely the work of driver Wayne Bilick. He and Freddy Watson spent weeks on the earlier Common Sense Revolution tour asking reporters what they expected from the campaign bus, and what would make life easier for them. As a result, desks at each work station were equipped with reading lights and a cell phone and computer hook-up at each seat. At the rear was a kitchen with microwave, fridge, an electric wok, and a seemingly never-ending supply of pizza and bacon on a bun.

Gone were the days when the bus had to stop to allow each

reporter to file. Now they could file as the bus rolled. And the Tory bus was almost always within cell phone range of Toronto. Only once was the leader's bus not in contact with the University Avenue party headquarters. That happened during a last-minute swing through northern Ontario to Bancroft. When HQ lost its electronic tether to the campaign bus, workers likened it to a spaceship disappearing to the other side of the moon. They knew it was there, but they couldn't reach it.

The New Democrat media bus, on the other hand, was a torture chamber. It was clear that the party cared not one whit about comfort, food or whether reporters were able to file their stories. And news outlets suspected from the soaring bills which they were getting from the NDP campaign that the party was attempting to use media outlets to fund their tour. In the first week of the campaign, news outlets received a $3,000 bill for airfare on top of the $5,000 which they were charged for a seat on the NDP bus.

The Tories charged a flat fee of $5,750. The Grits charged $5,050, which covered the costs of all travel, including airfare. Reporters paid for their own hotels and meals aside from the couple of light meals which the buses provided each day.

Press Gallery President Richard Brennan, a columnist for the *Windsor Star* and Southam News, remembered his employers' shock when they received a bill for $8,000 from the NDP after the first week of the campaign. The NDP charged airfare over and above the tour price, and they charged the commercial airline rate plus 10 percent, Brennan recalled. One day the NDP flew from Kingston to Ottawa, a distance easily driven in an hour or so, and they charged media $700 for the flight. And the New Democrats treated the media dreadfully on the tour. Brennan recalled that *Toronto Star* reporter Lisa Wright went for thirteen hours one day without food. There was no food on the bus and there was no food on the plane.

"The NDP continued to treat the media the way they did in their four-and-a-half years in government. They treated them like garbage. They drove them all day and didn't give them anything to eat." Eventually, after Brennan was quoted in the *Toronto Sun* complaining about the way the NDP were treating media, the party improved things slightly. But it left a bitter feeling among many media types, especially when the NDP's inflated bills arrived. The shocks on the NDP bus were shot. There were no fixed desks. Reporters had to balance their laptop computers on bouncy flip-down tables that made it impossible for them to work.

Meanwhile, the other two parties charged the media a reasonable rate and probably ate some of the cost themselves. After all, the political parties do have to make the election tour. The plane is going to fly to Kapuskasing, or Windsor, or wherever – no matter what. Having the media aboard just makes the economy of scale more effective.

"The NDP was mad at the Press Gallery. They blamed their entire demise on the gallery. It was all our fault. How could we have been so negative?" Brennan said. The Tories, on the other hand, made no mistakes when it came to dealing with the media. Brennan covered all three campaigns, and while he realized exactly why the Tories were coddling him so cleverly, they did make life easier and more comfortable for him.

"It was amazing. We were on the road for forty days. You didn't go home – and I was putting on weight," Brennan said. And he quoted one Tory insider: " 'The dumbest thing you can do is lose an election because you don't have enough Cheez Doodles.'

"We're human like everyone else. And if we're not being fed, and if we're not getting time to eat and it's just go, go, go, you can get cranky. And that crankiness, whether you like it or not, is going to come out of the end of your fingers."

For all the hard work, there were lighter moments on the bus. After all, grinding out stories for forty days from a bus puts a lot of pressure on reporters. Brennan did a stand-up Elvis shtick. CBC's Raj Ahluwalia taped a version of Chain Gang, which he played loudly as a background to the Tories' workfare plan. Brennan remembered doubling over with laughter when Ahluwalia, who is of East Indian background, prepared for an event at the legion hall in Bancroft. It was the second event at a legion hall in two days, and Ahluwalia disappeared into the bathroom at the back of the bus and emerged with his head swathed in a toilet paper turban.

"I think I'm ready for the legion," he said in his best Peter Sellers accent, making reference to recent controversies in which turbans were banned from some legion halls.

The 1990 Tory campaign, Brennan recalled, was a "disaster." But they were smart this time around to treat the media not just professionally but humanely. Many in the media appreciated Tory steadiness. Even when they were down in the polls, they remained calm.

Tory wagonmaster Gord Haugh is a veteran of political buses. He still has an itinerary from Robert Stanfield's 1972 campaign, and he "dabbled a little" in the Bill Davis campaign of 1971. Times have changed, he pointed out. In those days, with no cell phones and no laptop computers or satellite trucks, the advance man's job was to find a room at every stop with ten or twelve telephones for reporters to use. He worked for Kim Campbell's campaign, Jean Charest's Ontario campaign, Brian Mulroney, and Joe Clark.

As far as political campaigns are concerned, Haugh's seen it all. He knows what it's like to win big and to lose big. A campaign that is going down the tubes is no fun. The Tory campaign in 1995 resembled the Mulroney free trade campaign – it had a mission statement, a bold agenda set out for all to see.

"We went into the free trade campaign and in the first couple of weeks it started to go into the dumper," said Haugh. "Nobody got discouraged because everyone knew we were saying the right thing. If we were going to go down the tubes saying the right thing, it wasn't going to bother us a lot. And we went from 12-15 points behind with two weeks to go and we turned it around and pulled it out."

Of course, in the free trade campaign the Tories were the government. But the idea of having a message and a mission was similar.

"We went into this one way behind. We knew we had the right message, we knew we had the message the public wanted. Our underlying numbers were good. We just had to go the course. So one of the key things we worried about was, when the criticisms inevitably flew, would our candidates, our team, be prepared to go the course?

"In 1993 [the federal Kim Campbell campaign], when things started to go wrong, everyone got off the ship. I'm not saying we would have won in 1993, but if we had hung together as a team, we would have done a lot better than two seats."

During 1994, Haugh helped test drive the Common Sense Revolution around Ontario. He remembered that the label Progressive Conservative was still unpopular in Ontario, and that there was a movement at the 1994 London convention to bring forward a motion to change the name of the party.

After the May 1994 tour, Haugh was given the job of putting the bus together in a way that would make it easier for the media to do their work. Bus driver Fred Watson talked to several members of the media to find out what they needed. There were endless details to be worked out. The Tory bus, for example, had cell phone antenna poking up along the roof, giving it the air of some exotic temple to high technology. Haugh found that internal antenna really didn't work well enough and was prepared to sacrifice esthetic beauty for something that was more functional. They also used Bell cellular phones on the CSR tour and discovered that any time they were close to the U.S. border in places like Sault Ste. Marie and Belleville, the phone system would click over and they would be required to feed in an American credit card. That's one of the reasons why Haugh insisted on Cantel for the trip.

"I'm sure there are places where Bell is stronger than Cantel. But all I know is that it happened to us three times in a period of two weeks on the CSR, when we got to the Soo and when we were driving along the St. Lawrence."

Haugh even checked out a futuristic, hi-tech "communications in motion" system that's still in the experimental stage. It uses a radio signal to transmit from computers. It wasn't highly developed enough for this campaign, but watch for it in the 2000 election.

"The amazing thing about our bus – and I've never seen it happen in a campaign before – was that you'd pull up to a hotel and people didn't get off the bus."

In other campaigns, the media would make a beeline for the media room as soon as the bus pulled up at a filing spot. Occasionally, the bus would be parked outside Queen's Park, where most reporters had their offices, and they wouldn't even bother getting out of the bus and going inside. Reporters would be inside tapping away on their laptops.

Haugh was primarily responsible for making the buses work as moving offices for both politicians and the media. Indeed, everything worked so well on the day of the debate that the *Globe and Mail* bought three seats on the Tory bus so that their reporters could file from the CFTO parking lot.

Haugh simply thought things through better than the people on the other buses. He insisted on getting his bus to the station early to find a good location for cell phone reception, and in a master stroke of public relations, he invited all media who couldn't file from their assigned buses to come and file from his.

Over the years, Haugh has refined bus technology to the point where he has it down to a fine art. Photocopiers, for example, are extremely useful on the road but are very tricky to keep operating. The toner slops around when the buses bounce. This time around Xerox lent the Tories a bubble jet fax machine for the bus, which turned out to be a printer, photocopier, and fax machine all in one. He ended up using two of those instead of a photocopier.

Although the media appreciated the lengths to which the Tories had gone to make filing easy, it was the kitchen equipment that made life on the bus bearable. A microwave was inevitable. And a fridge. And then it was decided that an electric wok would be just the ticket, along with a toaster – after all, reporters do like those toasted bagels – and a teapot, because Bob Reid, the Tory media person assigned to the bus, preferred tea to coffee.

All this catering led bus driver Freddy Watson to comment that once upon a time the media was happy with beer and a packet of chips.

"Now they want friggin' yoghurt," he grumbled, in his broad north of England accent.

Well, not quite. One reporter complained that she really didn't like the beer and asked if she could have a Corona. Quite simply, nothing was too much trouble for Haugh. Next stop, Corona magically appeared on the bus – with limes. There is only one problem with Corona: it is only available in bottles, not cans. If the bus had crashed, the media would have drowned in a tidal wave of Corona.

When Press Gallery President Richard Brennan complained that there was no bulletin board for his notices, Haugh was determined to pick one up before the day was out.

And then there was the gourmet dining. Haugh decided at the beginning of the campaign that he didn't want to rely too heavily on the cholesterol-laden burgers and fried foods the drivers used to buy from a truckstop. He became a gourmet cook, with the help of President's Choice. He discovered that he could buy a box of meatballs, cook them up in salsa sauce, and, voila, he had a tasty treat that was not fried or fast food. Or he'd buy a shrimp ring, or cook up some PC potato skins in the microwave oven.

"Everyone thought they had died and gone to heaven. It was not only healthier, it was cheaper," he explained.

After one particularly appetizing feast, Paul Rhodes, the campaign's senior media adviser based at University Avenue headquarters, got calls from the media raving about the gourmet delights which Haugh was serving up on the bus. They were salivating over bacon-wrapped scallops and Swedish meatballs. Rhodes phoned Haugh on the bus to ask what was going on. Wasn't he going just a little over the top, Rhodes asked. Haugh explained that it was cheaper and better than ordering in fast food. And he didn't miss a beat. "Anyway, that was last night," he explained. "Tonight is fajita night. And tomorrow we're doing fondue."

There were some touchy moments, of course. In early April, when rumors started to fly that Bob Rae was about to call the election, the Tories realized that their buses had to go in for their 100,000-mile servicing. As the buses sat, unpainted, in the garage, their guts ripped out, the Tories spent a very uncomfortable two weeks biting their fingernails, praying that Rae wouldn't call the election and leave them without buses for the first two weeks of the campaign.

Haugh remembered bringing the buses downtown from the Brampton shop which had done the striking decal work. They had to bring them back in the middle of the night and cover them up in brown paper shrouds so that the media wouldn't find them too early and ruin their intended impact. Unfortunately, the buses were also vandal-proof. The shrouds refused to stick to the surface. Eventually it worked. The bus was loaded and ready to go. All they needed was an election call.

Chapter Thirteen
Closet Politics

Throughout the election, the question of same-sex spousal benefits hovered around the edges, never quite taking centre stage, even though a handful of demonstrators tried their best to hijack the spotlight.

Voters had a clear picture of what they felt about extending adoption and insurance rights to gays and lesbians. In a curious way, it became a pivotal issue. It wasn't that a majority of voters agreed with New Democrat Premier Bob Rae that extending these rights was an important human rights issue. Far from it. On the Richter Scale of issues, same-sex benefits could barely raise a ripple across the province. Overwhelmingly, the economy, taxes, employment equity, welfare, and health care topped the polls as issues of concern.

What same-sex benefits came to represent, however, was Lyn McLeod as a flip-flop. The Liberals had made an embarrassing about-face on the issue. During a by-election in 1993 in the downtown Toronto riding of St. George-St. David, which has a large homosexual population, the Liberals promised to support same-sex legislation. But when Bill 167 arrived at the legislature, they balked. The Grits later explained that it wasn't the same-sex benefits that bothered them. It was the last-minute inclusion by the New Democrats of a clause that would allow gays and lesbians to adopt children. Whatever the reason for backing away from the issue, it hurt them. Voters like consistency – and fairness. Mike Harris consistently told voters that same-sex legislation was not a priority for him, and the vast majority across the province agreed with him. Even those who didn't agree had to respect his honesty.

McLeod and the Liberals, on the other hand, were seen to have exploited the issue unfairly to curry votes in the by-election, only to turn around and abandon the gay community when the crucial vote came in the House. Even though many people may not have cared about same-sex benefits, they did care about treating gays and lesbians fairly.

There were times, however, when it was difficult to be charitable to some of the demonstrators. One weekend, an OPP bodyguard assigned to Mike Harris was bopped over the head by an activist angered at Harris's "It's not a priority" policy on same-sex spousal benefits. It did make you wonder what planet these vocal demonstrators had been on for the last five years. Here we were, tiptoeing nervously out of the worst recession in living memory, and these guys are bashing people on the head over fringe benefits? Taxpayers were reeling from $4 billion in extra levies. Welfare costs topped the $6.8 billion mark, and these guys were worried about whether their lovers got their teeth cleaned for free? Spousal benefits for homosexuals aren't about human rights or discrimination. They are about middle-class, well-heeled whiners with comfortable jobs and benefits packages trying to milk the system.

Gay rights activists will tell you that they pay taxes too and deserve every possible spin-off. Whatever happened to the notion of the public good, that you don't necessarily get back immediately what you put into a fund – be it taxes or insurance premiums? But somewhere down the line, you'll pick up pension benefits or a disability cheque, or a you'll get your drugs paid for you if you become chronically ill.

We all pay taxes, but we all don't use publicly funded services to the same degree. What about the great number of workers who don't have benefits for themselves, let alone for their spouses? Few companies offer the kind of gold-plated benefits offered by government insurers.

Also during the campaign, gays and lesbians claimed victory when Judge James P. Nevins ruled that four lesbians were eligible to adopt their partners' children. It seemed bizarre that a judge would take it upon himself to strike down a law single-handedly, in light of the tussle in the legislature in 1994 when Bill 167 was defeated. Whatever happened to the supremacy of parliament?

People, not judges, should write the laws. Then again, giving the whole ball of wax to appointed judges would save a lot of money and all that inconvenience of having to hold elections every five years.

In reality, the adoption issue is a phony one, since gays and lesbians have been fostering and adopting children for some time. When it is in the best interests of the child, courts and children's aid societies have been placing children with homosexual couples. And, frankly, that's probably the best way to decide such issues – on an individual basis. There are many instances when a gay person might be the best person to care for a child. There are gay couples who would not make good parents, and there are some straight couples who shouldn't be allowed to adopt.

But the decision to change the definition of "spouse" surely should be made by the representatives of the people elected to the legislature. Heaven help us if judges are going to dictate community standards. But back to the campaign.

It was sad that a handful of powerful, predominantly white male special interest types could intimidate candidates and dictate the agenda of the election, masquerading under a "minority rights" banner. Gays and lesbians have the right to live, love, and work freely anywhere in this province. As a socio-economic class, they are financially powerful and a much sought-after consumer group, which has enviable amounts of disposable income. What they were demanding wasn't equality; it was a stake in the political arena.

On the other hand, ousted New Democrat MPP George Mammoliti was wrong when he said during the campaign that cabinet ministers should disclose their sexual preference. You can understand and sympathize with his frustration. He'd been ostracized, ridiculed, and hung out to dry by his own party. Perhaps Mammoliti believed that there were members of the NDP cabinet who may have had ambiguous sexual preferences and were behind the nasty little campaign that was waged against him from within party ranks.

But the fact remains that one's sexual proclivities should remain private. I don't want to hear about them, and I'm sure most voters don't. All politicians – cabinet members or otherwise – eventually have to answer to their constituencies on how they voted. Let them answer on the issues, not on their sexuality.

Meanwhile, Liberals completely mishandled the same-sex protest. At one demonstration at a Toronto film studio, a handful of people showed up dressed as flip-flops. Unlike the bop-on-the-head from the demonstrator at the Harris event, this was a non-threatening, even funny, protest. And yet local Riverdale candidate Frank Lowery completely over-reacted, accusing the protesters of "political terrorism." Media types were left scratching their heads on that one.

At the same time, however, you do have to wonder why Bob Rae kept dragging the same-sex issue out of the closet during the first week on the campaign trail. Perhaps, having run out of safe subjects, he turned to safe sex. He forgot that the great majority of voters don't give a hoot about same-sex benefits. But having destroyed our economy, reduced our legal system to a laughing stock, and turned welfare into a way of life for a large number of Ontarians, he probably felt that homosexual rights were probably the only issue on which he could make some mileage.

Then again, Rae had to be careful not to provoke a revolt among his traditional base of support within Metro, especially in the west-end Italian communities, including Mammoliti's. Those people lived according to traditional family values and didn't spend too much time worrying about the gay agenda. People who've had their income slashed during the recession, and who are struggling to pay their taxes and feed their families, are not too likely to welcome yet another divisive debate aimed at legitimizing the lifestyle of one more special interest group.

Spousal benefits were originally intended to cover society's poorest and most vulnerable – mothers and children. Women who stay home to raise their children take a tough economic hit, in lost salary, health benefits, and pensions. Older women, most of whom have dedicated a large part of their lives to raising children, are some of the poorest people in society. Without spousal benefits, they would be punished even more. Gay couples, meanwhile, usually have more disposable income and no children.

During the debate on spousal benefits, we were told that gay men needed spousal health benefits because many of them had AIDS and couldn't afford medication. However, when the province announced a new $75 million Trillium drug plan for the chronically ill, that argument quickly evaporated.

Bill 167 was debated and defeated. The electorate – at least those living outside downtown Toronto – wanted real solutions to the real problems affecting the economy, welfare, and the deficit. On election day, they made their voice heard at the ballot box. They chose a premier who said that spousal benefits were not a priority, and they rejected the Liberals, who had appeared to exploit the gay agenda for the sake of political expediency.

Farewell to all that. Ontario Premier Bob Rae prepares to hit the campaign trail outside Queen's Park shortly after he handed the election writ to Lieutenant-Governor Hal Jackman, 28 April 1995.

New Democrat bad boy Peter Kormos in a 1993 SUNshine Boy photo. Kormos was fired from cabinet for posing for this picture, but now says he was on the point of quitting over his party's failure to follow through on their commitment to public auto insurance.

Toronto Sun/Canada Wide – Jeff Harder

Getting the message out in a multicultural manner (Part 1). Bob Rae and aides don traditional Sikh headwear for a Sikh rally.

Denis Drever

Getting the message out in a multicultural manner (Part 2). Once the party of Wasp Anglicans, Ontario Tories made forays into multicultural areas in the 1995 election.

Toronto Sun/Canada Wide – Thomas Aoyagi

Clutching her Red Book and a gift of cookies, Lyn McLeod campaigns in Brampton, where the Liberals were obliterated.

Toronto Sun/Canada Wide – Warren Toda

Lyn McLeod and Mike Harris square off in the debate, 18 May. Immediately after the debate it appeared McLeod had won. In fact, Harris was the winner and McLeod was seen by some to be too aggressive.

Toronto Sun/Canada Wide – Norm Betts

A month or so into the campaign Premier Bob Rae took to the skies over Greater Toronto, hoping to point out to the electorate some of the NDP's accomplishments.

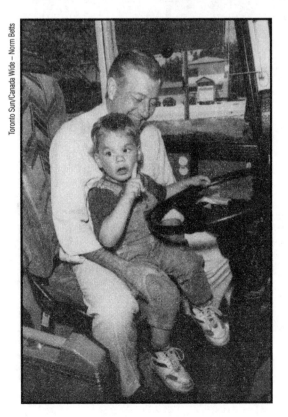

Toronto Sun/Canada Wide – Norm Betts

Taking control. Mike Harris and son Jeffrey take over the wheel of the campaign bus.

Mike Harris Sr. and son Mike take one last swing through Timmins.

Mike Harris Jr. takes over the camera from *Maclean's* photographer Peter Bregg during a cover shoot for the magazine at the Harris home in North Bay.

Denis Drever

Leslie Noble, Mike Harris, and Janet Harris cut 25 percent off a Queen's Park cake, representing the number of MPPs Harris plans to slash from the legislature.

Leslie Pace

A flatbed truck hauls away the 31 seats Mike Harris pledged to cut from the Ontario legislature.

Denis Drever

Mike Harris and the Tories announce an end to "corporate welfare" atop an apartment building in downtown Toronto, with the towers of business power as a backdrop. The announcement caught Liberals off guard. They thought he would announce his "workfare" program and came armed with statistics on welfare mothers.

Canada Wide/Toronto Sun – Mark O'Neill

Mike Harris and candidate Marilyn Mushinski poke holes in the Liberals' deficit plans, as set out in their Red Book.

Bob Rae might have hit some high notes on the piano, but he hit some off-key chords with unions and voters.

Mike Harris announces plans to end welfare fraud and cut benefits. Insiders suspect that a week of welfare announcements leading up to the debate may have been responsible for moving Tory poll numbers higher.

In the back of the leader's bus, where Mike Harris had an office complete with padded wing chair. *Left to right,* Deb Hutton, Mike Harris, Glen Wright, and Rod Phillips.

The Tory campaign team put their leader in numerous high-risk situations. Harris announced his controversial plan to end employment equity requirements at a multicultural high school in Scarborough.

Denis Drever

Woburn Collegiate students welcome Mike Harris to their Scarborough high school. He argued that students wouldn't need quotas to make it in the working world - and they agreed with him.

Leslie Pace

Videotapes were a hot ticket for the Tories. The party targeted undecided voters in the last few days of the campaign by distributing seven-minute videos highlighting local candidates. It was a highly successful strategy that Tories had test-driven in the Victoria-Haliburton by-election.

Tories made unprecedented gains in ethnic communities in the election. Here Mike Harris greets a voter in Markham.

Mike Harris, John Snobelen, and Janet Harris announce plans to slash school board bureaucracy outside the palatial offices of a school board in Peel. Snobelen became education minister after the election.

Gord Haugh

Mike Harris liked to recall in speeches how former Tory premier Leslie Frost used to view the province from a barber shop in Lindsay. Here Harris does some musing of his own amid the shampoo and hairbrushes.

Leslie Pace

Informality was de rigueur for the campaign team. The only exception was the day Harris spoke to the Empire Club, May 29, and the team duly showed up in suits and ties. Leslie Pace insisted she capture the moment for posterity.

Chapter Fourteen
Trust Me, I Can Do It

At the beginning of the campaign, Mike Harris had a big problem. Only his political opponents took seriously his promise to slash bureaucracy, hack welfare benefits, tighten up on fraud, and chop the income tax rate by 30 percent.

While Bob Rae and Lyn McLeod were busy drawing doomsday pictures of what a Harris government would do, voters weren't worried so much about what he would do, but that he wouldn't follow up on what he'd promised. They had become so disillusioned with politicians in general that even voters who liked Harris's get-tough plan were worried that he'd chicken out and not implement it. Even Tory polls reflected the public's cynicism. But Harris was adamant and steadfast that he would get tough. In an exclusive interview at the beginning of the campaign, he told me that while his plan was tailored to Ontario's needs, the province needed the kind of leadership which Ralph Klein had shown in Alberta.

"I think we do need a Ralph Klein kind of commitment for change that is appropriate for Ontario," Harris told me.

Harris blamed the credibility problem on a general disillusionment among voters who elected Liberals for change and got arrogance and who elected New Democrats on a platform of responsible government and got bungling, massive deficits, and more arrogance. What he heard loud and clear on the election trail was a plea from voters.

"People are saying, 'No we want you to be the same before, during, and after the election. Don't smoke us now.' They have been burned so many times in this way by politicians. And it affects all of us."

Voter cynicism in part prompted the Tories to release their Common Sense Revolution plan more than a year before the election. Traditional election strategy is to have platform unveilings at regular intervals during the campaign, but the Tories decided to take a radical stand and present theirs early and give the voters a chance to study it thoroughly.

It's proven remarkably endurable. So much so that once the Grits caught a whiff of the right-wing breeze that was sweeping North America, they drifted right along, attempting to claim territory which the Tories had already staked out. Harris said that his plan is more than workable and do-able. It's essential to returning consumer confidence and economic health.

"I believe the blueprint is there," he said, pointing to Klein in Alberta and Frank McKenna in New Brunswick as two models.

Harris mentioned some differences between Alberta and Ontario. While Ontario's deficit and spending problems are similar to those in pre-Klein Alberta, Ontario has a tax problem. Alberta had the lowest tax rates in Canada, which Klein was able to freeze and still stay competitive. Harris said that Ontario must cut taxes to become competitive once again. And while Alberta's over-spending was across the board, Harris said that in this province the bureaucracy became bloated at the expense of health care and education. He vowed to cut that fat and leave health care and schools untouched. He pointed to the enormous regulatory bureaucracy that has been put in place as a result of such meddlesome government policies as the new labor legislation and employment equity. Harris promised to slash red tape and reduce the layers of government for big savings.

Chapter Fifteen

With the Greatest of Respect

There are some pundits who are convinced that the turning point in the campaign came the day Tory campaign co-chair Tom Long looked straight into the assembled multitude of cameras and declared Premier Bob Rae and his New Democrats to be "irrelevant."

The media hordes were on hand to catch a first glimpse of the Tory campaign ads. Why, they wanted to know, didn't these slick Tory ads even mention Rae?

"With the greatest of respect," deadpanned the witty and oft-acerbic Long, "Bob Rae is irrelevant."

Although the statement came in reply to a media question, it was no off-the-cuff comment. The Tories needed voters to forget about Rae in the televised debate that was to follow within a couple of days. They wanted voters to concentrate on their leader Mike Harris and compare him to Liberal leader Lyn McLeod. And the strategy succeeded. Every TV station focused on that clip in the evening news, and viewers duly disregarded Rae in the debate. And once they focused on McLeod, they didn't like her.

"It was important to us," Long said, "because there were people, particularly financial people, who even though they might have wanted to support Mike Harris, the higher objective was to get rid of Rae, and if they thought splitting the vote was going to give Rae a chance, they were prepared to hold their noses and donate only to the Liberal Party. We needed to break the back of that."

Long also commented that it was vital to give the average voter, who wanted to vote PC but feared that their vote would let the NDP run up the middle, an alternative to vote their values. Rae was finished anyway.

"It was also an honest answer to a question. There was a very good reason why we didn't mention Rae in the ad. There are laws against necrophilia in the province, and there are very good reasons for that," Long quipped.

The advertisements themselves proved very telling. It was a strange peep-show, that hot spring afternoon. Hordes of media people swarmed from the seamier side of Yonge Street to a suite on University Avenue to a Cecil Street Union Hall, all sweaty for the latest clips. No, they weren't anxious to catch the latest dirty videos. It was political corn, not explicit porn, that was being peddled, as the three parties unveiled their paid advertising.

The Grits racked up no stars for their snoozer. It was supposed to be about balanced budgets and economic development. It was more like "Fairytales from Granny's Red Book." A warm, kind McLeod sat on a throne-like chair and spoke gently to us about what her Liberal government would do in thirty days, ninety days, and a year. It's hard to believe that the Liberals blew $1 million for production and airspace. They formed their own production company, Red Trillium, which sounds vaguely subversive, to produce the ads with Vickers and Benson. They were dreadful.

Boring is such an inadequate word when it comes to describing them. They should win an award from Insomniacs of Canada. If these didn't put you to sleep, try a sledgehammer. At the time, Grits said that they'd get tough if the opposition got tough. Which was perhaps the first indication of how they'd misjudged this campaign. Did they really expect the Tories and New Democrats to sit back and offer the same weak tea to the voters?

Not likely.

The Tories got two stars off the bat for making an effort to be multicultural, not usually a Tory specialty. They had voice-overs in Italian, Greek, and Chinese. The narrator sounded like Mike Harris, but it wasn't Mike Harris. He took the viewer through the merits of tax cuts and the need to abolish employment equity laws.

Their most effective ad was a brief, brilliant spot that compared Tory and Liberal policy.

"You won't hear Lyn McLeod talking about mandatory workfare," intoned the narrator, and immediately launched into Mike Harris's platform. The idea came originally from McLeod's own lips, said the Tories. Before the election writ was dropped, the Grits released their move-to-the-right financial policy, which in essence was a pale imitation of the Common Sense Revolution. The following weekend, McLeod went on Global TV's "Focus Ontario" and told viewers that you wouldn't hear her talking about working for welfare. The Tories immediately picked up on it and turned it into a stunning advertisement.

In the final weeks of the campaign, the Tories fielded a weathervane ad that depicted McLeod turning in the wind on issues. That, too, proved highly effective. This time, it wasn't McLeod who gave the Tories the idea, but another friend of the Liberal Party, the *Toronto Star*.

"Frankly, it's the only thing we can thank the *Toronto Star* for," said Tory campaign chair Tom Long. It was inspired by a 1994 editorial cartoon on same-sex benefits.

Jaime Watt and Amanda Walton co-chaired the Tories' advertising committee, although it was very much a group-think with the rest of the campaign.

"We decided early on that we wouldn't spend the bulk of our money on production. We wanted to spend it on 'buy,'" said campaign co-chair Leslie Noble. "You can't mix your message. The power of advertising is that you've got to be repetitive, you've got to really saturate your message, because that's the only way it's going to get across in all the clutter of all the political advertising. We did our own media buy specs, we defined the markets based on the number of seats in different areas, and biggest bang for the buck. We sent the media buyers out, Thomas Watt, which is Jaime's firm to do the media buy. It was all prepared so that the minute the election was called all the requests went out. We had all of our spots locked up within six hours of the election being called and I think that helped in a big way. The others were scrambling and they hadn't even got their requests in."

Jaime Watt co-ordinated the bulk of the creative and production work, and Amanda Walton focused on the buy and the riding liaison work. Padulo Advertising produced a lot of radio spots.

The principle that simpler is better was crucial to the Tory message. "The more you convolute your message, the more messages you're going to have, the less impact you're going to have," said Noble. The Tories spent $1 million on advertising.

Meanwhile, at the Steelworkers Hall on Cecil Street, the NDP came out swinging with their own version of "Bobby Sings the Blues." They attacked Lyn McLeod by attacking the federal Liberal government, asking "Whose side is she on?" The ads even got into the touchy issue of Rae Days, and explained that if they hadn't asked civil servants to take a few days off, they'd have been forced to cut 40,000 jobs "as the Liberals did." This was a clever way of blaming provincial Liberals for a federal act.

Ah, well, what's a Grit between friends?

Probably the most effective NDP ad was the one showing a maple leaf turning into one of the stars in the U.S. flag. It appealed to the anti-American sentiments expressed by many NDP voters. It was precisely the kind of hard-hitting, no-holds-barred ad you'd expect from a party which was running third everywhere in the province.

The NDP got extra stars for getting the most bang for their buck. Their total advertising budget was $750,000, which probably meant that we didn't get to see their ads as often as we did the Tory and Grit ones. But the NDP probably could have hit most of their supporters by focusing on "Star Trek." Beam 'em up, Bob.

Chapter Sixteen
The Young and the Hip

They're young. They're hip. And – what's most surprising – they're Tory. Although the team that pulled off the stunning turnaround in Tory fortunes could not be called political neophytes by any stretch of the imagination, nevertheless they were not your typical Conservatives. They were not your old school tie set. Come to think of it, they didn't belong to any kind of tie set. Informality was the key in the University Avenue headquarters of the Tory campaign. It was a thirty-something team of political upstarts – and a dog named Dave – who breathed new life into the Big Blue Machine and hauled it out of the political wilderness where it had been rusting for a decade.

Central players in the Harris team were campaign co-chairs Tom Long and Leslie Noble.

Outspoken and witty, Long had locked horns with some of the movers and shakers within the old guard of Tory-dom. A Sarnia native with a law degree from the University of Western Ontario, Long is proud of his blue-collar background. His father is a retired Dow chemical worker and his mother a homemaker. Long is passionate in his belief that the Tories need to return to their small "c" conservative roots if they want to appeal to people such as his parents and consolidate the 1995 election victory. Once considered something of a bad boy among the Bay Street elite of the party, Long has mellowed somewhat from his early days. His acid-like wit has been tamed to a gentle, self-deprecating humor, which can break up a roomful of the surliest media types.

Noble is an unassuming thirty-three-year-old cancer survivor. She brought the same single-minded focus to the job of electing Mike Harris that she used to battle the deadly disease. On the surface, she's quiet and self-effacing. But inside, colleagues said, she's made of steel. And once Noble has set her mind to accomplish something – like electing a premier – she usually gets her way. She used to work with long-time Tory backroom organizer John Laschinger and now has her own consulting company.

Campaign secretary Mitch Patten is thirty-seven years old and a native of London, Ontario. He cut his teeth in politics when he took a year off school to work in a junior job in Premier Bill Davis's office.

Alister Campbell, who is thirty-four years old, is an economics wizard from Kingston. He has a degree from the University of Toronto, a master's from the London School of Economics, and an MBA from Wharton in the U.S.

At the heart of the Tories' University Avenue headquarters was the ninth-floor "bullpen." It boasted exercise bikes, a putting machine, and computer games to calm frazzled election nerves. There was a dining room with catered meals, which workers paid for, and even a place to nap. Noble, Long, and Patten all had desks in the main office, while their assistants all had their own offices. Central to the set-up was the hotline, a speakerphone with a direct line to the Mike Harris bus. About the only hard-and-fast rule of the campaign was that this line had to be answered before all others. It was engineered to produce a different ring. The aim was to answer it within two rings, in order to provide speedy service to the leader.

About the only thing you couldn't find in the bullpen was a pinstripe. Directing Mike Harris's 1995 campaign was a different breed of Tory. This was the right wing of the party, which had been out of favor during the Red Tory years of Bill Davis and Larry Grossman. In many ways, they were quintessential conservatives who had never wavered in their views. It was Tom Long who first enunciated the right-wing agenda when he was a campus Tory. He and his allies were determined to do something which the Tories hadn't done for a long while – win.

There was only one minor mutiny during the campaign. It happened when Long's cocker spaniel, Dave, who was the campaign mascot – complete with his own photo ID – got into a bag of leftover Swiss Chalet chicken. Long and his wife, Leslie Pace, who also worked on the campaign, banished the dog from campaign HQ. Outraged staffers launched a "Free Dave" campaign. E-mail messages protesting Dave's exile flashed around the campaign's computer system, and "Free Dave" posters popped up everywhere at headquarters. It all culminated in a noisy demonstration at Long's desk. Campaign workers brandishing "Justice for Dave" signs humbled Long into submission and forced him to return Dave to his rightful place at the heart of the campaign.

The team's loyalty to Dave the dog may have provided some light moments during the heat and hustle of a political election, but their loyalty to Mike Harris and his Common Sense Revolution was anything but light. It was sure, steady, and solid.

"Five years ago Mike Harris made it his personal mission that he was going to win the next election," said Noble. "He was going to earn the respect of the electorate and he was going to represent their views. In order to do that we had to collectively jump through a lot of hoops. We had to reacquaint ourselves with the grass roots of the party."

Noble described the team as "a bunch of best friends working together. It was so much fun. It's such a tightly knit group.

"You didn't get the finger-pointing around the table. When a decision was taken, there may have been people who agreed or disagreed, but once it was taken, everyone was behind it.

"I'll bet it was a bit different over at the Liberal campaign," she said. Rumors of internal strife at the Grit nerve centre started circulating right after their sudden drop in the polls, although the Grits claimed that there was little infighting during the campaign.

Noble wasn't comfortable talking about her struggle with cancer. "It's a jinx to talk about these things. You're never 100 percent sure … there's never a cure," she said. It was her intense will power that allowed her to endure four months of painful chemotherapy and still keep her business going. She persuaded the hospital to let her go out and return each day without having to be readmitted every time.

Curiously, Long, Noble, and Patten all came to the "Mike Harris table" after having worked for different factions within the old guard of the Tory party. Patten had worked for Bill Davis. Noble had supported Larry Grossman. Long was a Frank Miller man. In the second leadership race, Long backed anyone but Grossman. He had fought bitterly with the long-time health and education minister. Finally he lent a hand to Andy Brandt, ensuring he became interim leader.

"I was sort of a pain in the ass to Bill Davis during that period," Long confessed, "not just because of the position we took, but because we were pretty persistent and forceful in making our voices heard when it wasn't really the Conservative thing to do.

"We agitated for a more conservative party and, on a political organization basis, objected to the fact that the party had a small, tightly-knit clique of people who seemed to run everything and who, in our view, increasingly became detached from both the grass roots of the party and, ultimately, Main Street Ontario."

Long supported Mulroney in the 1983 federal leadership and worked briefly in Ottawa for the former prime minister. Like a number of the young people who went to Ottawa at that time, he returned disillusioned.

When Long ran for party president after long-time incumbent David McFadden quit in 1986, Grossman backed Long's opponent. Long set off across the province to meet with the grass roots of the party. The Tories hate to use the word "reform," but that's the kind of movement which Long was hoping to start within the party. He ran on a platform that included moving the executive around the province, opening up lines of communication, and making sure that policy debate was more active.

Long wanted a renewal conference for the party. He went head to head with Grossman in a meeting with the caucus and party executive over how the renewal process was going to take place. Long recalled that Grossman wanted a blue ribbon panel.

"I felt that would just resemble the people that got us there in the first place," Long said.

Long won the debate. A party-wide renewal conference took place in November 1987 and was instrumental in passing major constitutional changes that opened up the party. It instituted a one-member, one-vote election process for the leadership of the party; it democratized fundraising and finances; and it insisted on a business-like board of directors.

Leslie Noble, meanwhile, was a long-time Grossman supporter. Ask the former Tory leader for an anecdote that will best typify how dedicated and driven Noble is to the task at hand, and he'll launch into the story about how Noble convinced him to take a second run at the Tory leadership. As soon as Grossman heard the news at his Muskoka cottage that Frank Miller was about to resign, he phoned Noble in Toronto and told her that he wasn't going to run. Within two hours, Noble was at Grossman's cottage. After she had wrangled a deal for office space with the help of an Orillia stockbroker, she persuaded Grossman to call key supporters and ask them to keep their powder dry, in case he changed his mind and decided to run.

"She told me I owed it to her and the other loyal workers to leave the option open and to make sure the team didn't break up to join other candidates who would declare immediately," Grossman recalled. Three weeks later, he still hadn't decided to run, but Noble already had his organization in place.

"I ultimately decided to run," said Grossman, now a partner in the law firm of Blaney McMurtry.

One of the people closest to Harris is his principal secretary, thirty-seven-year-old David Lindsay. The son of immigrant Irish parents, Lindsay grew up in Ajax and came to Queen's Park after a stint with the accounting firm of Price Waterhouse. Lindsay is a quiet and circumspect man. The media were fond of comparing his mild manners to those of the flamboyant Tom Long. In fact, the two are good friends. Despite their contrasting styles, they respect each other immensely. Lindsay joined Harris as his principal secretary shortly after the premier won the leadership race. He was at his side throughout the campaign, a calm hand in sometimes turbulent waters.

Despite the shifts within the party, there's still a bond of respect between the old guard and the brave new Tories. Both Grossman and former Tory premier Frank Miller worked on behalf of several candidates in the 1995 election, with Grossman putting in long hours stumping for Isabel Bassett in his old riding of St. Andrew-St. Patrick in Toronto and helping Emilia Valentini in Lawrence.

Miller admired the Harris team's bold strategy of putting out the Common Sense Revolution a year before the election.

"It was a huge gamble – they weren't sure where the people were. But it's stood the test," Miller said in an interview. He saw the fall of the old guard and the rise of the new Tories as a cyclical thing.

"It's what happens when a party is in power too long. And we were in power too long. I was sad to see it happen in my time, but you tend to lose the purity and edge after you have wallowed in power too long." Those who are left are more committed. The party is "purer." He added, "You're left with young idealists who are saying, 'I believe in this party no matter what. Even if it's not going to win, I'm going to work for them.'"

And Miller can sympathize with McLeod's sudden drop in the polls.

"I think basically it's a personal thing. People don't want to say that, but all of a sudden, Lyn was getting a lot of exposure. Even devout Liberals realize she isn't a very saleable character.

"I say that because I wasn't particularly saleable myself.

"I never enjoyed politics. That sounds crazy, but I enjoyed the responsibilities that came with being elected. But the game of politics was one I never understood – I think that was evident – I never understood the posturing.

"I'm an engineer. Engineers don't posture."

It's something the hip, young Tories probably would agree with. And so would Dave the dog.

Chapter Seventeen
A Blue Lady in a Red Outfit

The lady wore red. Power red. Liberal red. Red Book red. The shade of red that pundits said would sweep the province on 8 June. That was what the polls told us would happen. The media arrived at the debate, mid-point in the campaign, hoping that one of the three leaders – preferably McLeod – would goof and set a spark under a campaign which had been lacklustre at best.

All she had to do was hold her own, we were told. So long as she didn't trip up, she would win. It was up to Mike Harris and Bob Rae to derail the debate. In a strange sort of way, the Tories already had. A couple of days earlier, at the launch of their new and quite brilliant TV ads, Tory campaign chair Tom Long had looked straight into the television camera and told the province that Premier Bob Rae and his New Democrats were "irrelevant." He had condemned them to obscurity. It was a powerful notion to plant in the public's mind. And it worked. Viewers tended to disregard Rae during the debate. The leader of the ruling party, the premier of Ontario, the guy who'd been making the decisions in the big fancy office at Queen's Park for the past five years, had become an afterthought, an also-ran in the election. He was there, sure enough, warbling away in the background. But the election bus had left him standing on the sidewalk, scratching his head.

Of course, we all had known in our hearts for the past couple of years that Rae and his scandal-plagued government were not going to win another mandate. But Long spelled it out for them.

Curiously, Rae played along with the notion during the debate. At a pause in hostilities between Harris and McLeod, he interjected in a mild-mannered way: "If I could interrupt this lovers' quarrel." No doubt the image that he was trying to project was that he was the only statesman among a bunch of squabblers, but he ended up looking like an outsider.

Despite the fact that TV honchos had issued a no-props edict, McLeod insisted on taking her Big Red Book of Fairytales into the debate, and she flapped it around, à la Chrétien in the federal debate, at every possible moment. She performed ten Red Book waves, according to an informal count among media assembled in the lobby of the CFTO studios in Agincourt.

Mike Harris's goal was to convince the public that his plan would work, that the math involved in cutting taxes and balancing the budget really did add up. McLeod had to get voters to believe that the Tory plan wouldn't work and that the Liberal agenda was moderate and credible. Premier Bob Rae ended up, as he put it, mediating a lovers' tiff. His game plan was to show that neither the Red nor the Blue book added up, that no tax cuts were possible. So there was McLeod scolding Harris about "wacky" tax cuts, and there was Harris wondering what was so wacky about cutting the income tax rate by 30 percent, and there was Rae on the periphery, looking like a perplexed parent trying to mediate a spat between two wayward kids.

The timing of the debate was ironical. It was scheduled to take place on the evening of the same day of the opening statements in the Paul Bernardo trial. On any normal news day, nothing would be higher up the news schedule than a leaders' debate. But this was no average day. The Crown attorney's opening statement depicted such horrific crimes in so much graphic detail that news about the debate was pushed aside. Some observers felt that many viewers were so numbed by what they had heard on the nightly newscast, that they would not be able to pay much attention to the debate. In retrospect is seems that the TV audience did not give the debate their full attention until near the end. That's when a TV interviewer asked McLeod about her apparent flip-flop on same-sex benefits. And that's when she lost a lot of people.

Overall, Rae didn't perform too badly. He knew what he had to do and he did it quite well. He, too, had to poke holes. So he pursed his lips and looked suitably grave and told us that we couldn't have tax cuts, wacky or otherwise. He slammed McLeod's plan to end the 5 percent tax on auto premiums as giving the "biggest tax breaks to the people who have the worst driving records and the biggest cars."

However, it all came down to trust and leadership and all those things which Ontarians had done without for so long. Sure, the malaise went much deeper than a disgust for the New Democrats. We voted out David Peterson's Liberals because we were sick of two-faced politicians who said one thing to get elected and then did something else once they were in office. But how could Rae stand there and talk to us about trust in government when it was his regime that has caused the greatest betrayal? How could he look voters in the eye after doubling the debt, after Rae Days and the social contract, after introducing the most restrictive labor legislation in North America at a time when most people were just happy to have a job?

After the debate, the media concluded that there had been no winner. And if no-one had landed a knock-out punch, that meant McLeod had won by default. "She wins as long as she doesn't goof" was the media's mantra. On the day following the debate, most media pundits – and I include myself in that number – declared McLeod a winner. How wrong we were.

It was the beginning of the end for the Liberals. No one is exactly sure why. There are any number of theories, of course. One claimed that voters hadn't been paying attention to the leaders until the debate. Another was that she didn't look good on same-sex benefits. Still another was that McLeod was shrill and rude when she kept interrupting Mike Harris, in the process turning off voters in droves. There was also speculation that the Red Book hurt her. You can only use that kind of prop once. And every time she waved the book, she reminded voters of Jean Chrétien's broken promises.

No matter what the reason, the evidence became clear from all the polls and focus groups – by the time the debate concluded, Liberal support dropped like a stone in water and never came back to the surface.

Chapter Eighteen

Shout at Your Spouse, Lose the Election

I t is generally agreed by Grits and Tories alike that there were no defining moments in this campaign. There was nothing that came close to the federal Tory advertisement ridiculing Jean Chrétien's appearance. The debate changed many minds, but not because Lyn McLeod dropped some dreadful clanger and changed the course of history. It was all much more subtle than that. The debate was pivotal for reasons more complex and unfathomable than most people can actually put a name to.

But the Spouse in the House incident, as it was dubbed, was as close as it got to a defining moment for McLeod. In a swing through the southern Ontario town of Port Hope, McLeod made a policy statement on spousal abuse, and what she would do to punish partners who are abusive. McLeod told reporters that she believed courts should be given greater powers to ensure that abusive husbands – not their families – are forced from the family home.

Under the Family Law Act, before a judge will order the offender out of the house, a spouse must produce police or hospital records of physical abuse. McLeod said that the Liberals wanted to do away with this requirement and make it easier for the victim to prove abuse. The Grits would change the law to allow third parties, such as marriage counsellors, to give proof of verbal, psychological, or physical abuse. A woman could ask the court to throw the man out, whether or not she was seeking a legal separation or divorce.

Reporters pressed McLeod on what she meant by abuse, and McLeod told them that she would include verbal abuse in that category. *Sun* reporter Antonella Artuso summed the policy up in a lead-off paragraph: "Yell at your spouse and lose your house." It had a neat little rhyme to it and reappeared as the front-page headline of the *Sunday Sun*.

It was a turn of phrase that caught fire, and pretty soon it was the hot topic on talk shows. Within three days, McLeod had ripped off a letter complaining about the headline, arguing that the *Sun*'s coverage "belittles" and "trivializes" the problem of spousal abuse.

In the meantime, much to the dismay of the Grits, the story grew legs and walked all over the province, showing up in places in southwestern Ontario where the *Sun* doesn't shine. Liberal strategists suspected that the Tories were using the story in their canvassing, since it was appearing everywhere.

It came just at the wrong time for the Grits, hard on the heels of the debate, when voters were starting to focus on the campaign and the party leaders. All of a sudden they knew that the Liberal leader was a woman who made this silly statement about punishing men for the crime of yelling at their spouses. After all, people asked, what happens if both husband and wife are yelling at each other at the same time? Do you move both of them out and hand the house over to the dog?

"My proposal clearly applies to verbal and psychological abuse. It would not, as you imply, apply to yelling," McLeod said in her letter to the *Sun*. Except, isn't that what yelling is? Isn't it verbal abuse?

"Obviously, the courts would not give a spouse exclusive possession of the matrimonial home unless there is clear evidence of abuse," she wrote to the editor.

It was too little, too late, and spouses in houses haunted McLeod for the rest of the campaign.

While some Grit strategists still complain about the headline and the effect that it had on the election, the Tories claimed that it caused barely a ripple.

"It didn't show up in our numbers anywhere, it didn't get mentioned in focus groups anywhere, but it was one of those ways that people understood that Lyn McLeod didn't get it," said one Tory insider.

"People don't draw conclusions from a headline like that. They put stories together. They are much more sophisticated than campaign people give them credit for." Voters were more likely to compare her "shout at your spouse" statement to her condemnation of the Tories' plans for boot camps for young offenders and arrive at the conclusion that in a Liberal Ontario, if you shout at your spouse, you lose your house, but if you are seventeen and beat a sixty-eight-year-old pensioner to death with a tire iron, you get counselling.

Mike Harris committed his share of mistakes. The first, and biggest, blunder happened late one night when he announced that he would hold a referendum on the Windsor casino. The *Windsor Star* jumped on the story, and Tory candidates in Windsor went into a tailspin. Campaign co-chair Tom Long spent the better part of the next day on the phone smoothing the ruffled feathers of Conservatives in southwestern Ontario. Fortunately for the Conservatives, the damage was localized to the Windsor area. Moreover, the southwest is hardly a Tory stronghold, and many of their people were running as sacrificial lambs anyway. It was mostly an image thing, and the Tories moved quickly to contain it.

"Our guys down there rallied," recalled Tory campaign co-chair Leslie Noble. "You can either back down in the face of criticism, or you can say, 'This is what I believe and this is why I believe it.' He [Harris] had to do that.

"The candidates obviously felt strongly on the issue, because that's their area. But Mike has always said that this is an issue where you are free to believe what you believe on either side of it. That's the whole point of a referendum. In an issue like this, it is divisive, it does mean a lot to a community, one way or another, and the candidates just wanted us to know where they stood on the issue.

"It helped that so many people were willing to talk to them and take their opinions into consideration and were willing to help them verbalize their opinions. They weren't told to shut up and toe the party line. We said this is a referendum, no one's going to uni-laterally close down Windsor unless Windsor approves of it. So get out their and fight for your casino.

"Once they realized it was not business as usual with party headquarters and party leaders, they were actually pretty happy, because they got support. Even though there might have been a dif-ference of opinion over policy, they were actually allowed to speak their minds and to represent the community."

Harris's off-the-cuff remark about university tenure was widely reported and duly tut-tutted over by academics in university cities such as Waterloo and London, but it had no negative impact what-soever on the campaign. Actually, it may have helped the Tories. Several young professors phoned PC offices and said, "Right on!" With so many unemployed, and so many workers feeling insecure about their jobs, blue collar voters were angered that a small elite had guaranteed jobs for life. Although professors and others within the post-secondary education community put forward very valid and historic reasons for tenure, such as the guarantee of academic freedom, their concerns meant nothing to the average voter. Harris's "gaffe" probably won him votes.

Chapter Nineteen

Playing the Percentages

I t was the biggest shock of the campaign. Tory campaign workers rubbed their eyes in disbelief when they saw the headlines
in the *Toronto Sun* on the Tuesday after the Victoria Day weekend. Conrad Winn, chairman of COMPAS, an Ottawa-based
polling company, had workers out in the field collecting data in the
wake of the leadership debate the preceding Thursday. And the
results of the COMPAS-SUN poll were stunning. The Tories were
within a hair's breadth of the Liberals and clearly had the momentum going into the home stretch. They were within four points,
plus or minus a few, of catching the Liberals.

Naturally delighted to be doing so well, the Tories nonetheless
were a little nervous. It was too early for this to happen. According
to their tightly scripted program, this wasn't supposed to occur
until the following week. They didn't want to be seen getting too
excited or too cocky for fear that an unfavorable poll would come
out a few days later and take away that momentum.

Polls are a bit like fresh fish, however. The longer they sit on
the shelf, the more likely they are to smell. This poll was fresh.
Winn's workers had been busy all weekend, and the *Toronto Sun*
chose to report its findings immediately rather than wait for the
next weekend. The newspaper caught everyone off guard.

"The turning point was the leadership debate, in one sense,"
said Winn. "The measurable turning point was the leadership
debate. I think that ultimately when all pollsters release their data
probably there's going to be a consensus that while some pollsters

may have measured opinion change as much as a week later, I think that was the key point."

It wasn't so much a change in public opinion, Winn suspects, as it was mismeasurement by pollsters and misperception on the part of journalists.

"In many ways, the voters weren't with the Liberal Party for weeks, months, and years beforehand, it's just that they said they were.

"When people aren't really thinking carefully about how precisely they're going to vote, if you ask them how they're going to vote they're likely to say Liberal because they are the least disliked party," he said.

He made the analogy of someone who is busy working on a carpentry project. He is asked by a family member if he wants a Coke, and he gets a Coke. But the fellow doing the carpentry was preoccupied when the question was asked, and he gave an answer that he normally would not have given. "But that's not what I wanted," he finally says. "I wanted a cup of coffee or ginger ale. You know I don't drink Coke." If the Coke-bearer points out that he said yes to his question about the Coke, the carpenter will respond, "Oh, but I just wanted a drink."

"It's kind of superficial responding to simple survey questioning and I think that explains why the pollsters, including ourselves, measured such strong Liberal support. It was just a superficial thing."

Journalists, he said, are "almost uniformly, welfare state small 'l' liberals of some sort.

"In their personal convictions, they don't really believe in free markets too much and couldn't believe that Harris was at all credible. Quite apart from any polling data, they just didn't believe he had a chance.

"Harris was Mr. Polyester suit from a bygone era."

Also, said Winn, many Tory voters weren't saying, or just wouldn't admit, that they were going to vote for Harris.

"You had large numbers of people who politely claimed they were undecided when they weren't. Right up to election day, the last published polls were underestimates of Conservative support.

Because it was not 'politically correct' to vote for a Harris Conservative.

"That's not unusual. Quite often there are patterns when people are too afraid to admit how they are going to vote. That's why in Quebec there's a tendency, clearly shown in the 1979-80 referendum period, for the polls to underestimate the federal vote, because it's not politically correct, it's not fashionable, to be a federalist in Quebec. And it's not fashionable to be a free market conservative in Ontario.

"So there were people who wouldn't admit it and said they were undecided for that reason."

What counted for Harris, said Winn, were his policies. They were in touch with the electorate. The vast majority of media, including the *Toronto Star*, *Maclean's*, and the CBC, according to Winn, are very much to the left of the electorate.

"Ironically, the ideological and intellectual sympathy of the press for the left hurt McLeod because they never took Harris seriously, assumed she was a shoo-in and therefore focused on her warts," continued Winn.

"Any mistake she made was magnified. They assumed if it wasn't going to be the Rhodes scholar [Bob Rae] again as premier, it had to be her. And in the name of the people, they had to keep her humble. And, of course, in keeping her humble, they kept her as Opposition leader. Their left-wing bias, ironically, subjected her to greater scrutiny than they might have preferred, with hindsight. But they didn't think for a minute that Harris could win, so they ignored him."

And in ignoring him, they inadvertently helped Harris in two ways.

"When he did burst on the scene at the leadership debate time, so much of what he said seemed so exciting and novel. It wouldn't have seemed exciting and novel if the press had been talking about it – which they hadn't.

"Finally, because the press couldn't take any of these free market changes that Harris was proposing at all seriously, they didn't subject him to the same kind of scrutiny that they would have otherwise. If the press were full of intellectual and ideological conservatives, they might well have asked him some tough policy questions, some of which, being a human being, he would have failed to answer effectively. But they didn't take him seriously," Winn pointed out.

They could not believe that Harris would win the election. And the same media types probably will not believe Winn's conclusion that the most important big picture issue to come out of the election was that half of Ontarians think like U.S. Republicans.

"Here we have in Ontario, the centre of the Canadian cultural industry, and in Toronto, the centre of the anti-American Anglo-Canadian nationalists, writers, journalists, commentators, and thinkers, and the disjuncture between the reality of Ontarians, half of whom think like Republicans, and the image of Ontarians and Canadians as believers in a welfare state, it's just amazing the gulf."

So what can we learn from this election? Winn has some surprising observations. In a sense you don't need polling to understand Ontarians, he said. Half of the Conservative voters whom he polled didn't want a tax cut, and this is consistent with Americans. Republicans don't want a tax cut either.

"Just as Republicans in the States, Harris Conservatives in Ontario wanted their politician to act as if he wanted to give them a tax cut," Winn said. "There are so many similarities. I think that the intellectual leadership of the province, the cognoscenti, went into shock."

Then there was the role of the media. In the dying days of the campaign, when it became clear that the Tories were about to sweep to power, the *Toronto Star* started running outlandish headlines on their front pages predicting dire consequences for the province if Harris became premier. While Winn hasn't done any research on it, and while the *Star* is unlikely to pay him to do any, he speculated that the headlines may have hurt the Grits.

"While the *Star*, the big-hearted paper, would assume that most Ontarians would stand by single mothers and other unfortunate subsegments of society, that's not how the electorate would react. Maybe the electorate would say, 'Hey it's about time that the beneficiaries of the welfare state get a little nervous about all the goodies they get.'"

Early in the campaign, there was a story in the *Star* on money squandered on public housing.

Winn commented: "I don't know how the *Star* could think that the faithful readers of the paper would necessarily vote for Liberals or New Democrats after reading about the billions squandered on public housing."

Maclean's magazine made no mention of the COMPAS-SUN poll. It barely documented the rise of the Harris campaign and chose instead to run endless doting pieces about Lyn McLeod, the brilliant student and supermom.

The Liberal response to the poll was truly shocking. They blamed everybody and everything from the *Sun* to the pollster's sample size. Winn scoffed at their criticisms and said that any Liberal who believes bigger is better when it comes to poll sample sizes should apply the same principle the next time they have a blood test. In the interest of accuracy, they should ask the nurse to extract a gallon of blood instead of only a vial.

The Grits put out an internal campaign document that was breathtaking in creativity, but a tad disingenuous in some of the points that it made. Granted, it was a party piece, designed to keep workers in good cheer. Such pieces tend to get over-wrought in their partisanship.

"The *Toronto Sun* is running a poll which suggests that the election race has narrowed to within four percentage points. This result is simply not credible," the paper intoned. And it set out what it called "key points" for discussion.

"Our internal polling shows that the Liberals continue to lead in every region of the province, although they are in tough fights in central Ontario and parts of the Metro belt," it continued. Well, the Metro belt comprises 65 percent of the province's population. If you're in trouble there, you're in big trouble.

"Anyone who bets their mortgage on these results better have a lot of money to burn. This poll is a joke!" exclaimed the paper derisively.

It went on to question the number of people polled – 507 – which included 381 decided voters.

"This sample simply can't be counted on to draw credible conclusions," said the Grit spin paper. Well, actually there was a conclusion to draw from it, and it was this. Focus on the undecided voters. That's what the Tories did – to great effect.

The Liberal damage-control document was truly bizarre in places.

"Angus Reid's last province-wide poll, published in the *Toronto Sun* just before the election call gave us the support of 46% of decided voters, with the Conservatives at 28%, the NDP at 21%, with other parties at 6%." The Grit spin doctor continued, "This is the true benchmark for measuring poll results in the final drive to election day."

What an incredible statement. The Liberals had acknowledged all along that the gap would be closing. In this document they called it "a narrowing of the vote." Yet when it happened, they weren't prepared for it. Instead, they wanted the newspapers to continue using a six-week-old poll.

"Our internal polling shows that a plurality of people thought nobody won the debate, followed by those who thought Lyn McLeod won, those who thought Bob Rae won, and finally those who thought Mike Harris won," the Liberal paper continued. And in this belief, they were correct. Right after the debate, the media declared McLeod the winner. But focus groups, which the Tories and others conducted later, showed otherwise. Harris won hands down, they discovered, especially when he talked about trust. McLeod's popularity plummeted, and she alienated voters when she tried to explain her party's position on same-sex spousal benefits.

As soon as the Grits put out their document declaring the Toronto COMPAS-SUN poll to be in error, Liberal strategists started buttoning their flak jackets and pulling on their helmets. It had become an election war, and they decided that it was time to open up a second front.

Of course, they'd never admit in a million years that it was the COMPAS-SUN poll, the one they sneered at earlier in the week, that had caused this change in tactics. But you can bet the farm it was true. It was, after all, the first published poll to show the gap closing. By that time, the Liberals' own pollster, Michael Marzolini, was showing a catastrophic drop in Liberal fortunes after the debate.

Lyn McLeod and the Liberals finally ceased worrying about Bob Rae and his party, and turned their guns on Mike Harris and the Tories.

"We are going to subject Mike Harris's Common Sense Revolution and his announcements to significantly more scrutiny than we have been," Liberal campaign director John Ronson told me a few days after the COMPAS-SUN poll. "Your poll, I can assure you, had nothing to do with our change of strategy. Like other parties, we do internal polling. We have made our own assessments. Mr. Winn may think we should take advice from him, but frankly we are quite happy to take advice from our own pollster."

In fact, Winn himself told the Liberals that they still could win the election, and he offered some friendly advice and sound strategy for them to follow. For one thing, he told them not to panic. It was silly of the Liberals to blame the pollster and the reporting vehicle when their own numbers started to slide.

Another sign of desperation was McLeod's use of the word "wacky" at every opportunity. The Tory pledge to cut taxes was "wacky," we were told. The Grits claimed that Harris was going to cut taxes by 30 percent, when, in fact, the Tories had pledged to cut the provincial income tax rate by 30 percent. There's a big difference. And that wasn't "wacky" at all. It's a reasonable, fair, and equitable way to lower taxes for all income earners in the province.

But wacky is as wacky does. And some of McLeod's policies registered pretty high on the wacky scale. She announced that she would restore tax rebates on accommodation and purchases for tourists to the province. Somehow it's "wacky" to give residents of the province a break on their provincial income tax, but it's a good idea to give a tax rebate to people who don't live here? And "Shout at your spouse, lose your house" was "Open your mouth and put your foot in it."

The Grits said they were targeting specific tax cuts. First among them was the 5 percent tax on auto insurance premiums. Why give a break only to car owners? McLeod and her advisers were clearly clutching at straws. Meanwhile, the Tories were having a bit of fun at her expense. In response to her, "wacky" statement, they handed out T-shirts that read, "Call me wacky, I'm for tax cuts."

As the days passed and other polls confirmed the COMPAS-SUN poll, McLeod and her handlers became more and more desperate, at one point putting out a press release slamming Harris's commitment to welfare reform. That was a strange move. Harris's policy was absolutely clear and unassailable. The more he repeated it, the more support the Tories attracted to their cause. He said that he would cut off welfare to the able-bodied who weren't willing to work. McLeod had waffled so many times, no one was quite sure where the Liberals were. They came up with a convoluted plan called "mandatory opportunity." Voters suspected that their goofy plan was really mandatory opportunism.

No one was sure what their promises were.

Except, of course, wacky.

Chapter Twenty

The Dreaded Red Book

The Red Book was supposed to act as a sword and a shield. As a rapier, it would cut the Common Sense Revolution to shreds. If it didn't prove effective in the cut and thrust of the campaign, the fall-back position was that it would become a shield, warding off accusations that the Liberals had no policies. But the Red Book missed its mark. It was neither a sword to thrust at the Tories nor a shield to protect the Grits. Instead, the Red Book turned on its owners and cut at the heart of the Grit campaign.

The federal Liberal Red Book in 1993 went from being a shield to a sword. Jean Chrétien would say, "It's time for a change." That wasn't terribly revolutionary or original, because that's what Opposition leaders say. Kim Campbell and the Tories would reply, "Oh, you can't trust them." And the Grits would come back flourishing their Red Book. "Look, you can trust us, this book shows what we're going to do. It also shows that we have changed and we are not like we were in 1988, let alone like we were in 1984. We've got a new approach, it's intellectually solid. It's real. It's different. It's a shake up."

Chrétien easily turned his Red Book into a sword because the Conservatives badly flubbed the whole issue of having a plan of their own. The Red Book became a powerful weapon that Chrétien could use to slice and dice the Tories. And use it he did, to great effect, night after night. He'd go up on the podium and hammer them with his Red Book.

Books, plans, contracts, policy platforms – call them what you like – have become de rigueur, unless you're the New Democrats who ran a no-promises campaign in the last provincial election.

The McLeod Liberals, however, mishandled their own Red Book. It certainly didn't work as a sword, and it failed to function as a shield. It was supposed to deflect accusations that the Liberals had no plan, that they were fuzzy and mushy on issues. It was supposed to provide the details, but the voters weren't interested.

"It turned out it was a sword and it was pointed at us," recalls one Grit insider. It turned on the Grits because sometime during the spring of 1995, the Red Book became a symbol of incumbency, of the status quo. And people were telling the Grits that the federal Red Book was a symbol of broken promises.

Divorced from Chrétien, and divorced from the success of the federal government, the provincial Red Book was hardly a plan for shaking things up. But, having committed themselves to the Red Book strategy right at the beginning of the campaign, with costly ads ready for distribution, the Grits had crossed a Rubicon of their own making. There was no going back. They were tied to the Red Book for the duration of the campaign. The media sniggered every time they dragged it out.

It was also a question of ineffective marketing. The Liberal message went nowhere. Nothing came off the pages and grabbed voters' attention, and there are points in the Red Book that could and should have been used to better advantage. Welfare could have been dealt with more clearly. The Liberal position was a serviceable, politically effective, and conscientious stand. But it didn't come through. The deficit plan should have been tougher. It too died on the page. The Red Book was a vast mass of detail that really amounted to very little.

Liberal ambivalence was the only thing to come across clearly in the Red Book. For instance, they wanted to balance the budget, but they promised massive spending on subways and GO Transit. It didn't make sense. The Grits had been caught astride an uncomfortable fence, going from the tax-and-spend era to a balanced-budget policy in the space of four years. It stripped the small "l" liberals as well as the big "G" Grits of their ideological transmissions.

More importantly, it caught their leader off balance. Lyn McLeod didn't come across as a person who got into politics to balance budgets. She came to accept that balancing a budget is what you have to do and she acquired an impressive fervor about it. But her heart and soul weren't in it. The media sensed her lack of genuine commitment. The voters sensed it too. She made all the right speeches, went through all the right motions about balancing budgets and fiscal responsibility, but the bottom line was that it wasn't at the core of her political being, and everyone knew it.

Mike Harris, on the other hand, had always been a fiscal conservative. The tax fighter moniker had stuck to him during the 1990 election. He didn't have to go through any ideological contortions to find it.

"Just because you've got a Red Book doesn't mean to say people are going to vote for you," pointed out David Lindsay.

"I think they misinterpreted what happened in the federal campaign. Red Book versus no book was what happened federally. Kim Campbell didn't have a clear message of what she was selling, and Chrétien did. He said, 'I've got the people and I've got the plan.'"

And that was the crucial difference between the two campaigns. McLeod went from campaign office to campaign office showcasing candidates and the Red Book. The Tories chose to run on issues. They went into ridings and told people how bad the welfare rates were in their town.

In hindsight, would the Liberals still use a Red Book? Good question, remarked Grit campaign co-ordinator Bob Richardson.

"Should we appear to have modelled it precisely after the federal one? That's a fair question. I'm not sure that's what we should have done again. It was seen to be the standard that was set, and in actual fact, maybe we should have packaged it in a different way. What happened to a certain extent was we didn't get any of the benefits for putting out our own book. Whether you like it or dislike it or agree with the policies or not, it is a pretty substantive, well-put-together document. I think most people would acknowledge that. But we didn't get the benefits of that and we got the negative of those who don't like the federal Red Book or who didn't think X, Y, Z promise had been kept.

"So in actual fact we didn't get the benefits and we got a lot of the negatives," Richardson admitted. And he said that any future Liberal books will be in a different color and probably a different format.

This election showed that political parties have to communicate both less and more effectively. The Liberal campaign press releases proved the truth of this. They were long and tended to get bogged down in tedious detail, or they patronized the media by telling them what they should think on issues. The Tory releases, penned by Peter Varley, never went past one page and were often no more than half a page.

Why did the Red Book turn voters off in droves? It's hard to put a finger on exactly what it was that made people dislike it so intensely. For one thing, it was a mass of facts and figures and promises. For another, its timetable seemed designed to appease a cynical electorate. It was an almost exact steal from the federal plan. And it was predictable. The Red Book strategy had worked well for Jean Chrétien, and provincial Grits assumed that it would work well for them, too. How wrong they were.

Even the launch wasn't particularly well thought out. Lyn McLeod and the Liberals chose to unveil the Red Book at a posh Yorkville hotel. Before the press conference was over, wags were calling it the Four Seasons Revolution. It became the Truffles manifesto. So much for the common touch.

McLeod's Red Book was an unintended parody of Jean Chrétien's Red Book. He waved his book and won votes. McLeod waved her book, and people laughed under their breath and wondered why the Liberals were trying to foist something so transparent on a sophisticated electorate. McLeod's Red Book was dutifully Liberal Red, both on the cover and in content. It was small "l" liberal with tax money, too. If there was one special interest group left unbribed, it must have been the one whose votes weren't worth buying. They were going to build four subways which Metro Council already had deemed too expensive, and they were going to build the Red Creek Expressway in Hamilton and Hwy. 416 in Ottawa. And they wanted to extend Go Transit to Barrie, Peterborough, and Kitchener-Waterloo.

You want a subway line? You can have four. You want a GO line? Take what you want. Meanwhile, the Grits only budgeted $17 million in the first year and $4.2 million in each of the four subsequent years to pay for GO expansion. Their numbers didn't add up. It costs $6 million to build one kilometre of track. Where was the money to come from to build all those hundreds of extra miles? As for the subways, the Grits hoped to fund those "within the existing plan," according to one spokesman, "plus private funding." In fact, the Grit budget relied heavily on private partnerships, which seems bizarre. How can you balance a budget based on the notion that the private sector is going to kick in money? Or would the Liberals introduce legislation forcing companies to balance the budget for the government if the government couldn't do it alone? The Liberals expected the private sector to ante up $140 million in the first year and $1.6 billion after five years. Anyone who thinks that the private sector is going to finance subway lines should talk to former Scarborough mayor Joyce Trimmer. She thought that she'd secured private funding for the Scarborough LRT expansion, only to see it all fall through.

McLeod left few platitudes unturned.

"A Liberal government will be committed to excellence in learning," she told us. As if there's a political party in the world that will admit to being committed to mediocrity in education. When they were in office in the 1980s, the Liberals' great contribution to education in Metro was to force the entire school tax burden on property owners.

Of course, the Grits enjoyed the luxury of being able to walk on both sides of the street at the same time. They stole a plank from the New Democrat platform on capping trustees' salaries, a recommendation of the Royal Commission on Learning. But it was the Liberal government, in 1989, that unleashed trustees on the trough by giving local boards the right to set their own salaries. And it was the Liberals who added to the school bill by mandating heritage language classes, pay equity, and the employer health tax.

To add insult to injury, the Red Book stole the Tory promise to scrap the MPP pension plan and replace it with RRSPs.

But there were no cuts in income tax. They only talked about a

5 percent cut in targeted taxes. They told us that health care was sacrosanct. There would be no user fees. But they never got around to telling us why people wouldn't pay a nominal amount for something they profess to value so highly.

Their sole original promise was a vow to assign a cabinet minister for children's issues. It's about time government realized that kids' services have been sorely neglected. Those services are needed the most in hard times, but they're the ones that get cut first.

So there it was, in red and white. The great Grit platform. The Gospel according to Lyn, Our Lady of the Hustings.

If only they'd known that their Red Book plan didn't even have a prayer.

Chapter Twenty-one

Landslide Ernie

They used to call him "Landslide Ernie," the honorable member from Parry Sound, who first squeaked to victory in 1981 with a six-vote margin. Now they call him "sir."

Forty-nine years old, Ernie Eves is the second most powerful man in the new Conservative government. He is the other northerner. He thinks like Harris, acts like Harris, and understands where Harris is coming from. He even looks a little like Harris.

Mike and Janet Harris vacation with Ernie and Vicki Eves. They golf together; they socialize. It was natural, therefore, that Eves would be Harris's trusty lieutenant, the person who would implement the toughest parts of the Common Sense Revolution. And Harris raised eyebrows after the election when he placed Eves in not one but three high-profile jobs. First, he made him minister of finance, a key job in a government that has promised to slash spending, cut the provincial income tax rate by 30 percent, and balance the books by the end of its first mandate. Second, Eves is deputy premier. He is expected to step up to bat whenever Harris is unavailable. Finally, he is House leader, another demanding job, but one which Eves performed in the last session of the legislature.

Eves is confident that he can juggle all three tasks capably. His confidence was bolstered recently by a congratulatory note from former Liberal Finance Minister Bob Nixon, who held the same three posts.

Eves chuckled when he was reminded of the *Toronto Star*'s speculation on who would make it into a Tory cabinet. Eves's name was excluded. A number of his local supporters got very upset and phoned him and the *Star*. Eves tried to calm them down.

"The *Toronto Star* doesn't pick the cabinet, the premier picks the cabinet," he pointed out.

And Eves got a phone call from Harris at home that night.

"Hi," said Harris. "I see the *Star* didn't put either you or me in cabinet." And laughing, he told his long-time golf buddy: "We're both going to have to work just a little bit harder today to make sure we get there."

"The guy never lost his sense of humor," said Eves. "I think that's tremendous."

And people who try to stick Harris with "Chainsaw" epithets don't know the man, said Eves.

"Mike has two young boys at home. He's a very thoughtful, caring individual. If some media wish to portray him in another light, that's up to them. But that isn't the Mike Harris I know. He understands that there's a difficult job to be done and it has to be done. And I suppose maybe it's that determination that others want to portray as something else. But he is a very caring, thoughtful person. He's very much a family-oriented individual.

"Mike actually relates every situation or every problem he has to his family – how will this impact on my family? And I think that's the sort of philosophy that has got him where he is."

Eves subscribes to the theory that Harris the politician has been underestimated by his critics. He was at the 1981 nomination meeting for the riding of Nipissing. Even back then, Eves recalled, people were telling Harris that he'd never make it, that the riding had been a Liberal stronghold for twenty-two years. And yet he pulled it off. Harris did it, said Eves, the same way he approaches everything – in a businesslike, matter-of-fact way.

Eves had great praise for the young people who ran the campaign.

"Those people did a tremendous job. Tom Long is not only a very bright individual, he's also mature beyond his years. I know there was concern in some areas of the party, 'Are these young people, Tom Long, Leslie Noble, going to be able to do this?' And every time there was a serious problem or a political hot spot during the course of the campaign, Tom just took two deep breaths and a couple of steps back and, in a very relaxed, thoughtful manner said, 'What is the real problem here? Let's try to focus our energy on the message we are trying to achieve.' And he never lost sight of the goal, and Leslie was the same way."

As part of the Tory establishment, Eves admitted that in the back of his mind there was always a fear that the young campaign team might not be able to handle the stress.

"I've known both of them [Long and Noble] for a fair length of time. I suppose there's always this gnawing doubt in the back of your mind are these young people really going to have the maturity to deal with a serious problem when it arises, but having said that, they were not chosen by Mike in a cavalier, casual attitude. He put a lot of thought into what his options were and where he wanted the party to go and who was going to be best qualified to take them there. And he obviously made a very wise choice." The campaign was a team. There were a few over-inflated egos, but there was no backbiting or finger-pointing.

Eves sensed that the Liberals had at least two – "maybe more" – camps within their campaign, and this didn't help the Grits. "The perception I'm left with is that they weren't a cohesive unit all pulling together."

He was not surprised that the Tories did so well in the election. He underlined the fact that Mike Harris and other members of caucus spent a lot of time talking to people across the province.

"The Common Sense document quite simply reflects what people across the province told us they wanted. It represents four years research and grass-roots contact with the people of Ontario. So I don't think anyone should be surprised that it was overwhelmingly accepted by the people of Ontario.

"We realistically thought we had a very good chance of winning this election before it started. As a matter of fact, we had a transition team in place for months."

Eves was a member of that transition team, along with Harris's principal secretary, David Lindsay.

"I can't say enough about David Lindsay. I've known him since I first arrived at Queen's Park in 1981 and he's certainly grown quite a bit in those years. He's a tremendous individual." The transition policy was formed mostly by people who came and went and produced papers for the Tories on issues such as the bureaucracy, big government, and the appropriate number of ministries.

"Really, for that reason, I think we were able to hit the ground running on June 26. Some people are amazed that we were able to do what we did in the first four weeks. But there was a lot of hard slugging that went on behind the scenes in the weeks and months before June 26."

Eves claimed that it was his wide experience in both government and the private sector that convinced Harris to entrust three vital jobs to a long-time colleague.

"I'd like to think that I'm not here because I'm Mike's friend, although that is quite true, I am Mike's friend. We've become good friends. We first met in the late 1970s. We both shared a lot of common interests, and quite frankly, I think we think along the same lines," Eves commented. "I think it's very important that the premier feel confident that the person who is looking after the financial affairs of the province on his behalf thinks along the same lines that he thinks along. I don't think anyone should be surprised at that."

Eves was born in Windsor. His family moved to Parry Sound for a year when Eves was seventeen and then moved back to Windsor. Graduating from high school, he went to the University of Toronto to take a degree in political science, economics, and history. After two years he was accepted at Osgoode Hall Law School. He articled in Windsor and then bought a 50 percent share of a law firm in Parry Sound. Eves married his Parry Sound high school sweetheart, Vicki, and they have two grown children, Justin, who is twenty-three, and Natalie, who is twenty.

Eves was not politically involved during his years at university. He wasn't a member of the campus Tory movement that spawned so many of the architects of the Common Sense Revolution. His interest in politics began during the 1968 federal election. He became active in the local riding association, eventually becoming president. When the incumbent MPP announced a few days before the 1981 election was called that he wouldn't seek re-election, a shocked riding association had to hustle to find a candidate.

Eves was ready for public life.

"I've been a practising lawyer, I've done a lot of corporate and commercial transactions in the past, I know what it's like to meet a payroll," he said. "I know what it's like to go through the aggravation of payroll taxes and government red tape. I think Mike, in a different set of circumstances, has been through the same things himself."

Eves is a seasoned politician who brings considerable experience to the Harris cabinet. He has been chief whip, Tory House leader for five years, and a member of the Board of Internal Economy in the legislature. He is confident that he'll be able to keep his three high-profile portfolios, with the help of his two parliamentary assistants, Rob Sampson and Isabel Bassett.

The Ministry of Finance is now comprised of the old treasurer's office, the Ministry of Revenue, and the Ministry of Financial Institutions. The NDP rolled them into one. Sampson, a former vice president of the Chase Manhattan Bank, is the parliamentary assistant for financial institutions. He has been given the unenviable task of making sense of auto insurance. Broadcast journalist Isabel Bassett is working with Eves in his role as House leader, which will be a time-consuming but relatively familiar job for Eves. Bassett also is working with him in Finance.

Eves has run in five elections and has seen nearly every kind of voting trend. He really wasn't all that surprised at the apparently sudden turnaround in Tory fortunes.

"I've found in all the elections I've run in, initially the voters aren't really paying too much attention. When it gets two weeks away, they might start to think what they're going to do.

"Early on, there was no rapid movement in the polls. But once people got to understand that Mike Harris was not going to back off on what he stood for and once they realized that he was quite serious, that helped a tremendous amount. And the telltale sign was when the Liberal ads started to get negative and started to attack. They had a sense that they were slipping and slipping badly. And in fact, that's exactly what happened. They went into a free fall."

Eves said that the Liberal's two-to-one lead before the election indicated that their vote was "parked."

"When somebody phones you up and there's no election on the horizon, and they say, 'If an election were held today, who would you vote for?' well, you take what you think is a comfortable and safe choice. And Mr. Chrétien's been very popular federally and I think a lot of people without even thinking said, 'Liberal.'"

No one knew who Lyn McLeod was. When the campaign started, they still didn't know who she was.

"In the debate I think Mike demonstrated very competently that he wasn't flashy but he sure meant what he said and he was sincere in what he was talking about. I think that event at least brought home to the average voter that here's a guy who actually means what he says. We can trust this guy. And I think the election was in large part not only who was in tune with what the Ontario voter was thinking, that's what democracy is supposed to be all about, but also who can we trust to deliver on what they say they are going to do."

Eves says that the Tories' first months in power proved that they have every intention of implementing their platform. They will do what they said they would do.

"If nothing else, we have done exactly what we said we were going to do and we will continue to do that." What's more, the reaction he's getting from across the province is that voters approve of the cuts he's making. And he says no amount of noisy demonstrations on the lawn in front of Queen's Park will deter him from doing what needs to be done to get the economy under control.

"Part of democracy is that you have special interest groups and different groups that are going to try to speak up for their special interest. Having said that, we're here to deliver on what the majority of Ontarians want. And that's what we're going to do. And if that offends some people in the process, or if some people don't share the same political philosophy or point of view, well I'm sorry but we have to do what we were elected to do and it's very important.

"I think the future of this province depends on what we do economically in the next few years. I don't think there is going to be another chance for the Ontario economy to turn itself around. We are in a pretty serious situation with respect to debt and expenditure levels in this province. If we don't rein them in now, they're going to be out of control."

Eves started his career as a Bill Davis Tory, when the party was more middle of the road, more Red Tory than the current breed, but the new finance minister said that he is "very comfortable" with where the party is now.

"I think there are different governments for different times. In those times, the province was extremely well run and well managed, with all due respect to other governments. The government ended up being in power for forty-two years. Maybe at the end they lost contact with the people and they got their just rewards. Having said that, they did something right for those preceding years, otherwise they wouldn't have continued to keep getting elected. People can now appreciate in Ontario just how well the province was run for those forty-two years, as opposed to what they have had for the past ten. Unfortunately for us, we're left holding a pretty deep economic debt bag, that we're going to have to dig ourselves out of, but we are committed to doing it."

Eves said that the Liberal and New Democratic governments of the past ten years "thought they could solve every problem by throwing money at it. They didn't stop to think about whether they had the money to throw at it or where they would ever get the money. They just threw it at the problem. Everyone who runs a household or a small business can appreciate that it's not a revenue problem that is causing the province's financial woes, it's an expenditure problem. And until the government gets spending under control, we will continue racking up deficits and debts."

Eves said that the first thing the government must do is bring the deficit down every year until the books are balanced. As for the accumulated debt – the $90 billion or so racked up largely by the New Democrats – that's something they will have to attack further down the line.

"You also have to stimulate the economy. I think the last two governments have proved conclusively that giving away taxpayers' money for short or temporary make-work programs doesn't work. We got further and further behind with that kind of thinking. The only thing that is going to work is providing an economic climate in this province where individuals and business feel comfortable and want to locate. We have become very uncompetitive in our tax rates of all kinds, be they payroll taxes, employer health tax, WCB, the rate of personal income tax. We've become very uncompetitive and these people aren't stupid, they know that, so they go where the business climate is more suitable."

Eves wants to bring new industries to the province and has asked trade minister Bill Saunderson to look into the competing jurisdictions which deal with business.

Looking down on a remarkable view of the main legislative building, the "Pink Palace," from his seventh-floor office in the Frost Building, Eves pondered where he'd like to have the province's finances by the end of the first Tory mandate.

"At the end of our mandate, I'd like to introduce a budget in the year 2000 that will fully balance the annual budget of the province of Ontario. I think that's going to be a difficult goal to achieve, but I think it is an achievable goal with a lot of hard work. I'd like to have consumer and business confidence reversed to the point where they are optimistic and they want to locate and they want to expand in the province of Ontario."

It is indeed a tall task.

Attacking the deficit, balancing the budget, coming to terms with the $8 billion which the province has to pay to service the debt – all these things amount to a monumental task. It is like trying to stop the *Titanic* from crashing into the iceberg – when the berg's only a a hundred yards away. What's more, there are those who don't see any reason why the ocean liner *Ontario* shouldn't plunge merrily ahead, partying its way to a disaster.

Chapter Twenty-two

Whatever Happened to the Liberals?

S o what *did* happen to the Liberal campaign? Liberal polls showed that the nosedive began right after the debate. But was it Lyn McLeod's performance in the debate that caused the free fall in the polls? Or was it something else? Was it quite simply that they had never enjoyed the two-to-one lead in the polls that everyone had cited during the fall of 1994 and the spring of 1995? Perhaps that two-to-one figure was a figment of pollsters' overactive imaginations.

Clearly, the Grits were outmanouevred and outwitted by the Tories, whom they had grossly underestimated. One intriguing scenario compared the Tory kids to the Liberal kids. The Tories handed over their campaign to some very young people within their organization, and then they stood back and let them run the show. The Hugh Segals and the John Torys of the PC party may have wanted to dabble, but they had the good grace not to meddle. They held back and gave help only when asked for it. By and large, they realized that it wasn't their campaign. On the other hand, according to this scenario, the Liberal gray hairs did just the opposite. They handed their campaign over to the kids and then let the old guard, the movers and shakers within the party, stick their oars in at every step, telling the kids what they were doing wrong.

That's one scenario. Liberal Party president Richard Mahoney said that it wasn't just one thing that caused the Grit demise.

Tory advertising was far more effective. The "Shout at your spouse, lose your house" headline in the *Toronto Sun* had an impact. "It didn't turn around the campaign or anything, but it had a huge political impact," said Mahoney.

Essentially, there were three things that conspired to sink the Grits, said Mahoney.

First, the Liberals started the campaign with a 20-point lead which they'd had for more than a year.

"The jaws of the trap are set when that happens because the expectations among the public, the media, and yourselves that you are going to win are so high that you tend to start playing almost an incumbent style. People start to look at you as an incumbent and you start to look at yourself as an incumbent. As a result of that and a number of other factors, our message was qualified, and less clear than the Tory message was."

The Tories, Mahoney claimed, had no choice but to go out on a limb and run a "wedge" campaign. Welfare abuse, he said, wasn't an issue in their polling, but the Tories had identified it before the election as something that infuriated taxpayers.

"Everything we did was middle of the road. Liberals are by definition a centrist party. But a centrist party can't be confused with saying here's where the Tories are, here's where the N-dippers are, let's go in the middle. That's not what it should be about.

"So you had Harris on the one hand who was 20 points behind and needed to take some risks. It was a very clear, well-executed, shrewd campaign designed to stake out their ground."

Secondly, the Liberals had a qualified, fuzzy message, and they were trapped by the status quo snare. Thirdly, according to Mahoney's logic, as a result of the first and second points, it came across that the Tories stood for change and the Liberals didn't. The entire Tory campaign was about change.

"We misread it," he admitted. "Our campaign was designed, I think wrongly, to talk about credibility – all our fifty independent experts and all that sort of stuff, careful positions, many of them well thought out. Their campaign was about a clear message – let's change things." In that context, the Liberals ended up defending a "weaker version of the NDP status quo."

Mahoney said that it's unfortunate and ironic in many ways that this happened. McLeod does stand for change. She does want to change the way the government is run.

"Back in the leadership campaign she talked about how government interfaces with people, about making it more community-driven, more locally driven. I think that's the way politics is going. In ten years time, you'll have much more local democracy, much more direct democracy, and even some of the underpinnings of the Common Sense Revolution are more locally based, decision-making things. But it's not exactly the easiest thing for the electorate to latch on to," he predicted.

"Getting tough on welfare and getting rid of quotas is very simple. And people are in the mood for change. They don't have a hell of a lot of time to sift through your own baggage. You're going to have to do that for them, and we didn't do it."

Mahoney subscribed to the notion that there was no defining moment in this campaign, no single act or omission that caused Grit fortunes to tumble. But he does offer this insight into the outcome of the debate. On the morning of the leaders' debate, the Liberals were still at 49 percent, the Tories were at 30-31 percent, where they had been for a long time, and the NDP were at about 19 percent. Liberal polls had not registered a significant change from the day the writ was dropped. According to the Grits' own tracking, the Liberals dropped a couple of points during the weekend following the Thursday night debate, but the loss was not significant. On Sunday, the *Sun* ran the "Shout at your spouse, lose your house" story, and on the day after the Victoria Day holiday, it ran the COMPAS-SUN poll. By that same Tuesday night, the Liberals dropped 5 points. On Wednesday, another 3 or 4 points of support disappeared. On the following day they lost 2 more points, and on the Friday they lost another 2.

"Those days after the long weekend, that's when the Liberal lead disappeared," concluded Mahoney. He wasn't sure what triggered the week-long free fall, but several factors seem to have kicked in at the same time. First, there were the Tory ads, which were highly effective. By the Tuesday after the long weekend, their effect was working its way into poll results. Secondly, there was the debate. Tory focus groups during the debate showed McLeod doing well, until the last question on same-sex spousal benefits. That, too, may have hurt their leader. Following hard on the heels of that came the "Shout at your spouse" story, with the COMPAS-SUN poll two days later. One thing is clear – the Grits went into a tail-spin. It was a black week from they never recovered.

"We dropped something like 16 points in eight days," Mahoney recalled, although Tory insiders said that their polls had started to move before the debate.

Some election pundits thought that it was the cumbersome structure of the Liberal campaign that doomed it to failure. There were too many people involved in a complex, brokerage model of decision-making wherein everyone had to be consulted over every move. Nothing ever got done.

Mahoney, an Ottawa lawyer, co-chaired the campaign with John Ronson and Deb Matthews. As the campaign closed in on election day, the line of responsibility devolved to Bob Richardson, an aide in McLeod's office who was campaign co-ordinator with responsibility for message, polling, advertising, and so on. Ronson, who was campaign director, had responsibility for organization, tracking, etc.

During the election writ, Mahoney moved to Toronto and worked with the media and became the party spokesperson.

"I chaired an advisory group that we had meet once a week which was a bunch of big, Liberal Pooh-bahs who would come in and tell us what we were doing right or wrong. We were doing everything right, of course, in the first two or three weeks, and we were doing everything wrong in the last two weeks."

Mahoney admitted that the campaign was a "bit diffuse," but it was also manageable. As proof, he talked about the week the polls dropped.

"The morning of the COMPAS poll, I went on CFRB with Conrad Winn. That morning my marching orders were not to trash the poll but to raise issues about the small sample size and not to worry yet.

"By Wednesday evening, I was telling the media it was neck and neck. We actually made the turn in that forty-eight hours. In my view it was late. We should have turned before we had evidence the Tories were gaining on us. We always knew the Tories were going to catch up. We thought it would happen in the first eight to ten days.

"That's when we thought that people would focus and they would say, 'Hey there's a choice here!' and that we would drop 7-10 points and that big lead would disappear. And we would be into a slug-out. But it didn't happen. Eighteen days after the start of the campaign, we were still 20 points up."

When the polls didn't move at the beginning of the campaign, a lot of pundits thought that it was going to be a ho-hum, sleeper of a campaign, similar to the one that had taken place earlier in Saskatchewan.

"When it eventually did happen, twenty days into the campaign, we were probably a little slow to turn. On the other hand, I think what happened this time in Ontario was pretty fundamental," Mahoney said. Even so, he continued, the problems within the campaign may have been more basic than simply timing.

"I'm not sure turning two days earlier would have made much difference. We had message problems. I don't know why, but our leader just didn't connect with voters. I think she's an enormously capable person who could have added to the public life of Ontario. It didn't happen. But, much as I lament the fact that we didn't turn earlier, I'm not sure if we had turned it would have made a difference."

Voters had moved to the right. In so doing, they had cut out the Liberals, because when it came to issues of the right, Mike Harris had already claimed the ground. The Common Sense Revolution had begun to take hold. And there wasn't any ground there for the Liberals to hold. In fact, there was nowhere for McLeod to go but down. Bob Rae started to come on strong as Harris and the Tories gained ascendancy, leaving McLeod caught in the middle. At one point, about ten days before the vote, some polls showed the NDP at least tying the Liberals for the role of official Opposition. It was that bad for the Grits. All the traditional voting patterns in Ontario had gone out the door. They no longer could count on their traditional stake. They were a hair's breadth away from being relegated to third-party status.

Mahoney, who is thirty-six years old, said that there was some truth to the speculation that the Grit kids weren't left alone to run their own campaign.

"I don't know if it's quite that simple, but there is something in what you say. There is no question that finally, in this campaign, having followed the careers of some of the 'revolutionaries' and known some of them for a while, they've been held back by some of the Big Blue Machine, and they were the kids. And they finally had a candidate, they controlled him. From the beginning, they put the revolution together – and congratulations." If Mahoney thinks that "the kids" controlled Harris, he knows next to nothing about how Harris came to power.

The Tories opened up the party and let in a brash group of young people to run the campaign. And, what is even more surprising, they pretty well had a free hand. No matter what the reservations of long-time backroom workers may have been, they stayed out of it. The Liberals, meanwhile, had been comfortable letting Keith Davey and Gordon Ashworth run the party for twenty or more years.

"I don't think we've yet had the confidence in ourselves to totally let it go, and I think we should," Mahoney said. "Internally, it's an interesting issue. On the advertising side, Vickers and Benson have been doing Liberal campaigns forever. Federally, provincially, all the ones for David Peterson, all the ones before that for Pierre Trudeau."

Should the Liberals have toughened up their ads to take a more attack-style format? Mahoney wasn't sure. Attack ads might have backfired on the Liberals. They were perceived as the leaders, almost the incumbents, with a hefty lead in the polls. It would have been gross overkill for them to have come out swinging too hard against the Tories.

Mahoney told an interesting story about the Liberal ad that portrayed McLeod sitting in an overstuffed, throne-style chair. It was an obvious attempt to make her look dignified, in control, a person fit for the premier's office. The day it was released, he received a call from a Tory colleague telling him that one of the

first ads produced for them had originally taken a similar format –
making Harris look like a nice, dignified premier. But that wasn't
the message which they wanted to get across. They were 20 points
behind in the polls, and they had to come up with hard-hitting ads
about change.

"That ad was obviously designed to talk about credibility and
to make Lyn look like a premier," Mahoney said. "It was very similar, almost identical, to an ad Jean Chrétien used in 1993.
Chrétien's ads in 1993, I would argue, were not seminal to his success. The only ad that was important in 1993 was the Kim
Campbell ad that allegedly made fun of Chrétien's features. Ours,
in trying to make Lyn look credible, simply made us look like more
of the same. It had no impact. It wasn't that it hurt us, it just had
no impact. I just wished that either we had a harder message to hit
up, or that we had changed earlier. But the question is would any
reasonable person with a 20-point lead run an ad that would knock
the stuffing out of Harris? Everyone would see it as overkill."

Ultimately, said Mahoney, the election could have been won,
but the Grits had to learn that "it's not good enough to be the middle." And he quoted Pierre Trudeau when he said the Liberal Party
should be the "radical middle."

He's supportive of the federal Liberals and Paul Martin's fiscal
conservatism. During the Trudeau era, radical change took place in
social reform, constitutional matters, and language laws. This generation of the radical middle wants to get our fiscal house in order.
Until that happens, social change cannot happen.

"We need not just middle, we need radical. It cannot be that
just because we are a centrist party that we are afraid to take tough
stands," he said. He pointed to gun control. It is a tough, unpopular stand, but it is the right thing for the federal Liberals to do.
Similarly, slashing the federal budget isn't a popular thing to do,
but it's the right thing to do.

"I think we have to go back to Trudeau's original formula. It
will be a different application of it, but we need to be not just middle, we need radical.

"The trap that Liberals fall into, not just in our campaign, is
that because we're Liberals we tend to say, 'Well, let's find that mid-

dle path.' I'm saying that's the wrong way to start off. Let's find the right path."

Looking back at the operational side of the campaign, Mahoney saw things that he'd change. Campaign advertising was one. He admired the way in which Jaime Watt handled Tory advertising. Watt wasn't someone brought in from the outside. He was intrinsic to the campaign from the beginning and had a good feel for the message which the party wanted to get to the people.

"Rather than go to the advertising pros who have been doing it forever, I'd get a Jaime Watt. I'd get one person who I'd bring in. We lost sight of how important the message was. We were playing for credibility. This campaign wasn't about credibility, it was about change. People said, 'You are all equally incredible. I disbelieve all three of you equally.'

"We were no more credible than Harris, in fact in the end we were less credible. In fact, going in we thought no one would believe Harris," he recalled. "As well, internally, we needed a tighter group."

And the third issue was one which Mahoney felt deeply about and had difficulty expressing. It concerned McLeod and her leadership and why she failed to connect. And this was something that confounded many in the media who watched her. One-on-one, McLeod is a warm, intelligent, kind person, who listens to people's concerns and talks intelligently about them. McLeod the candidate became a captive of her handlers. She allowed herself to be cocooned by the multitudes of people around her. It appeared to reporters that she was incapable of speaking for herself. She had to go back to the campaign team and ask them what the Liberal message track was on everything. One reporter remembered looking at her through a TV longshot. She was a short, dumpy woman standing at the top of the steps, dubbed Mt. McLeod by the media. It was hard to imagine, the reporter said, why she was so far ahead in the polls. Obviously, voters saw it that way too.

"Part of it was gender," said Mahoney, "but it was more than that. Gender isn't the fundamental thing. I can't probe into people's minds on it, but I know that I watched it with Kim Campbell. I think we do hold women to a different standard than we hold men to. That doesn't mean that a woman can't win. It depends how much and what standard you are held to. And sometime holding women to a different standard benefits them."

Polling showed that as a woman, McLeod represented change and honesty. However, as a woman she also was seen as being less capable in matters of finance. But you have to wonder about the accuracy of such polling data. After all, was Margaret Thatcher viewed as being less capable with the nation's money because she was a woman?

Mahoney said that his greatest regret about the campaign was that the Liberals weren't able to get out to the public all of Lyn McLeod's good points – the warmth, the intelligence, the kindness.

"The most impressive thing about Lyn McLeod is the thing that can be most challenging in politics. She is an incredibly deliberate, cautious, thoughtful person. But I think those are all good qualities in a premier. I actually want my premier to think before he or she acts.

"She has an enormous gift to reconcile competing views, to bring them together and to a synthesis. She has an enormous gift to bring clashing parties together at the table. She actually fundamentally believes that government needs to be done differently. And I don't think we ever successfully articulated this." And she maintained her poise even as the campaign went down the tubes. There were no tears, no recriminations. McLeod was calm and classy. "And she's smart," added Mahoney. "I like smart people in politics. There aren't enough smart people in politics." McLeod's grasp of the incredibly complex financial platform and other tricky policy stands impressed him.

The finger-pointing and recriminations, however, began even before the election was over. Rumors swirled about Michael Marzolini, the Grit pollster. One rumor said that he'd been dumped by the Grits who were consulting Goldfarb. This was nonsense, replied Mahoney. He attributed the rumor partly to the Tories and partly to the old-timer-versus-young-kid theory. Goldfarb had done Liberal Party polling for years. Marzolini was a relative newcomer. His first campaign was Jean Chrétien's 1993 federal one.

"It never happened. We didn't dump him. That didn't happen," Mahoney claimed, although he admitted that Marty Goldfarb and others associated with his company did give some advice to the campaign.

"I think that what really happened there, though, was that the story came a little bit from the Tories and a little bit from the inter-industry competition that pollsters engage in." Stories at the time charged that Marzolini didn't provide tracking early enough in the day and that he had told the Grits to attack the NDP, instead of going after the Tories.

Marzolini also said that the stories were nonsense.

"In fact, in the election it was made very clear to all the candidates, and we did three candidate briefings on this, and to the campaign management, that the major opponents were the PCs. We said the PCs can be elected and the NDP cannot be elected. There was no possibility of the NDP forming a government. Things would have to really radically change in the province for that to happen. What we had posited, however, was that the PCs were not unpopular. There was little scope to really go in and attack, especially as a front-runner. A front-runner should never be running negative ads at that stage. However, because the NDP was an incumbent, you could use the NDP and attack the NDP to contrast ourselves – and this was the whole key to the campaign, we had to contrast ourselves – against the PC party. The PC party in effect did an excellent job of contrasting themselves against the Liberals. That, to a great extent, aside from the debate, is why they won."

Marzolini continued: "The Liberals could use the NDP as a foil to contrast themselves against the PCs. The NDP were hated. There was vitriol against the incumbent NDP government. They were a target that was welcome. So the Liberals therefore could attack the NDP with impunity but only if it advanced the cause of saying to the public, 'Look, this is what the NDP have done, which you don't like, we're going to do this, and we're going to do it differently from the PCs, because the PCs would do this and this is how we make ourselves different from them.' And that's the message that was delivered to the candidates and management."

Another rumor was that Liberal campaign management wanted to use negative advertising earlier in the campaign, and Marzolini advised them not to do so.

"It's always a mistake to run with negative advertising when you're 25 points ahead in the polls. There has to be a reason for negative advertising. The only time when you can use negative – and we prefer 'contrast' – advertising, is when the numbers are somewhat closer," Marzolini said. "Now, before the debate when the Liberals were well ahead, there was no need for contrast or negative attacks on the PCs. It would have been laughed at by the public.

"The PCs, like the Reform Party in the 1993 federal election, may not have been agreed with, but the people thought they were putting positive, constructive solutions, whether they were good or bad, to the public. And you cannot attack a party like that at that stage. When you should do that is when the numbers are closer. And it was our recommendation very soon after the debate that we start putting negative, attack ads together in order to basically do more to contrast ourselves with the PC party," Marzolini said.

And he scoffed at stories of late reports.

"We provided, on a daily basis, anywhere from a 10-20 page analysis of the data, we did that in two business hours, and that's faster than we did for Jean Chrétien in 1993 or David Peterson in 1985." Marzolini also polled for Elinor Caplan and Dalton McGuinty.

"Of the people we've polled for, all told, we've done 340 campaigns and 86 percent of those have been victories for our candidates. Although the kind of candidate that takes winning seriously is the type of candidate that comes to us," he pointed out. "They say, 'I want to know what the people in my riding are thinking so that I can react to what their needs and desires are.'"

In hindsight, Marzolini said that one or two executional things could have been done differently. But, he added, in the final analysis, the outcome of the election would not have changed significantly.

"Public opinion is civilization's most powerful currency, and the vote is an expression of that and it was quite decisive."

And he's quick to scotch other rumors about infighting and backbiting within the Liberal camp once the campaign started to fall apart.

"I didn't see any of that. Actually, Bob Richardson did a very good job of holding things together. Whenever a campaign starts going badly – and they're very fragile things, a little bit of pressure and it's turn the wagons into a circle and fire inwards – something Bob did was to hold that steady. There was no infighting – at least not until after the election."

One thing is clear. No one wants to go into a campaign as number one again. Bob Richardson said that the poll position had too much baggage. The leader in the polls often is seen as the incumbent and is therefore subject to immense scrutiny. Even though the Grits had acknowledged, prior to the campaign, that their massive lead was "soft," they too had come to believe the numbers.

"We always knew our vote was soft. But I think to a certain extent, no matter how hard you fight against it, you get a little bit seduced by the numbers. I've run a leadership campaign where we were number two and I've been involved in a campaign where we were number one going into it. Let me tell you, number two is a whole lot easier," Richardson said.

"You're looser, you're able to respond quicker, you move quicker. You are under less scrutiny from the media. And it's an easier position to move from. When you're number one, you're under a lot of heat. You're afraid if you do this or that it will impact on your lead and you tend to be more conservative. It's a tougher spot to be in. I think there is some truth to the fact that the support was soft. There was no reason to believe this outcome was going to happen. But there was no question that it was always a tighter race than the public and maybe the media perceived."

Richardson said that while their campaign structure may have been ponderous and slow to turn around, it didn't fold under pressure. He pointed to the hideous ad put out by a desperate Kim Campbell campaign in the last federal election as something his people didn't want to repeat. There's a huge difference between losing and still maintaining your position as official Opposition and being reduced to a mere 2 seats in the legislature.

"Nobody is entirely safe in Canadian politics any more. It's not a given that you'll come back with 30 seats. You could plunge down to zero or two if you really lose it and make huge errors," he remarked. "And you don't really want that to happen. So even if you're not doing well in a campaign, it's important to make sure that you don't make a colossal error, because there isn't that margin there any more. Who would have thought in 1987 that the Progressive Conservative Party could go down to 17 seats? If you had said that five years before that happened, you would have been committed. There's no cushion any more. You've got to be cautious and do the right thing."

Traditional voting patterns in Ontario simply don't exist any more. No party is guaranteed a predetermined share of the vote. While the Liberals managed to pull 30 percent out of the fire, the hard core Liberal vote is usually around 31 to 32 percent. Evidence abounds that had the election been held a week earlier, the Liberals would have been reduced to third-party status.

"I would probably suggest if you looked at who voted for us, it may not be the same coalition that voted for us ten years ago. We used to dominate in the south-west, now we don't any more. Now we do better among ethnic Canadians in parts of Metro."

The party, Richardson said, has more of an urban base in cities such as Metro Toronto, Ottawa, Sudbury, Hamilton, Windsor, and Kingston. Meanwhile, the Tories swept suburbia and did well in rural areas.

As for the future, Richardson continued, the party needs a "clearer, crisper" message. "We can't make people work to understand what we want to do."

One thing that could make rebuilding difficult for the Liberals is the fact that their platform was seen as merely a kinder, gentler version of the Tories'. They will have a tough time fighting the Harris government in the legislature. The Red Book will be the Liberals' albatross.

Speaking to the Empire Club, Mike Harris strikes a pose that recalls the history and ties of the old-style Tories.

At an event at a Chinese restaurant Mike and Janet Harris break open a fortune cookie with a message predicting a big Tory win.

Denis Drever

Confronted with demonstrators on Danforth Avenue in Toronto, Mike Harris kept his cool. His bodyguard was later bopped on the head by an angry protester.

Denis Drever

Mike Harris meets with local business people for a round-table discussion in Guelph.

Supporters hand Mike Harris a winning number at a rally in London.

Bus driver Freddie Watson gives Harris aide Deb Hutton a hug in front of the media bus.

The Tory buses turned heads all around Ontario with their striking decals designed by Lynne Atkinson.

Aboard the media bus was a microwave, an electric wok, a well-stocked fridge, and even gourmet dining.

Denis Drever

Harris aide Glen Wright and press spokesperson Bob Reid confer on campaign strategy.

O'Shea-O'Drowsky photo

Global TV reporter Sean O'Shea and news cameraman Mike O'Drowsky help entertain young Mike Harris on the long last leg of the campaign. The three became firm friends and O'Shea (*left*) and O'Drowsky even let the youngster try out their camera.

Tory wagonmaster Gord Haugh, a veteran of election campaigns from the Davis years, spent the forty-day campaign aboard the bus keeping media types well fed and making sure their stories made it to their assorted media outlets.

Mike Harris's bus had all the comforts of home and included a comfortable armchair, a cell phone, fax machines, and a team of campaign workers to keep him in touch with campaign headquarters in Toronto.

"Can you tell me the way to the legion hall in Bancroft?" CBC Radio's Raj Ahluwalia, upon learning that for the second day in a row the Tories would be holding a press conference at a legion hall, disappeared into the bus bathroom. He emerged with a toilet-paper turban and announced that he thought he was now ready to face the legion.

Leslie Pace

Tom Long's dog Dave was the official campaign mascot, complete with photo ID. He was banned from campaign headquarters, however, when he got into a bag of leftover chicken. Angry campaign workers staged a noisy demo at Long's desk, demanding Dave's return. In the end, Long was forced to capitulate.

Denis Drever

Glen Wright conducts the nightly tour meeting with Gord Haugh, Deb Hutton, Rod Phillips, and Bob Reid.

Leslie Pace

Each morning in the private "Bullpen," the Tory campaign team would go over every aspect of the campaign, from media reports to polling.

Leslie Pace, photo

Twice a week, Tom Long and Leslie Noble would hold conference calls with half a dozen candidates. Here they are seen going over numbers.

Law enforcement and boot camps were all part of the Tory platform. Here Mike Harris outlines the Tory get-tough justice policy outside a correctional facility in Ottawa.

Mike Harris's policy adviser, Deb Hutton, and his principal secretary, David Lindsay, put the finishing touches to the Tory leader's victory speech in Harris's rec room on election night.

The new and the old. Newly elected premier Mike Harris greets former Tory premier Bill Davis after the election.

Savoring victory on election night, Janet Harris gives her husband the thumbs up sign for a job well done.

Chapter Twenty-three
Political Orphans

If victory has a thousand authors and defeat is an orphan, the 1995 New Democratic campaign is pretty well all alone in the world. Few New Democrats were prepared to go on the record about what went wrong. One close Bob Rae aide angrily declined an interview for this book, and André Foucault, the party president, refused to say very much.

"We ran the best campaign we could, and we did a good job. Mechanically, it turned out very well and the voters responded other than we would have preferred them to and that's the end of the story. I'm just not prepared to analyze the campaign," Foucault told me in a brief telephone interview.

"Analysis is a question of perception and every person you talk to will have a different perception of the campaign. I am not prepared to open the debate or open the analysis for others to respond to," Foucault added. "I'm very satisfied with the way things went except for the result – that's the only thing that's missing, substantial though that may be in the equation."

However, what went wrong is all too obvious for party renegade Peter Kormos. By the time the election writ was dropped, the Tory campaign was pretty well over, and the fate of the New Democrats had been sealed. Kormos said that party brass refused right until the bitter end to concede that they were going to be dumped by the voters. Kormos maintains that the election was lost when the party abandoned public auto insurance in a decision taken at Honey Harbour barely a year and a half after the election of 1990.

"That was the beginning of the end," he said. Rae and the New Democrats had drawn some of their strongest support during the 1990 election campaign from people who supported public auto insurance, and backing down on it was seen as the greatest in a litany of broken promises. Among the average voter, public auto insurance was the issue most closely identified with the NDP.

Kormos, who was fired as minister of consumer and commercial relations when he posed as a SUNshine Boy, fully clothed and leaning against his bright red Corvette, said that if Rae hadn't fired him, he probably would have quit anyway, so unhappy was he on the auto insurance flip-flop. Kormos has dumped his once-beloved Corvette and now wheels around town in a Chevy truck. You can't help wondering if it's because of the insurance rates.

The NDP's penchant for alienating its traditional base of support became part of Kormos's political patter, by way of a joke he'd drop in speeches.

"There's a rumor going around that there's a group that meets every Monday morning in the premier's office to decide which group to piss off that week. That's not true. It meets every Tuesday." It may have been a joke, but there was a wealth of truth behind the quip.

The unions, especially public sector ones, the New Democrats' most reliable and most trusted supporters, were inflamed by the ill-thought-out social contract. And the private sector Canadian Auto Workers particularly were embittered by Rae's policies.

"We betrayed our own constituents," Kormos claimed. "It began with public auto insurance." There are some within the party who say that public auto insurance was adopted by the NDP just to be contrary to the previous Liberal government, as an expedient way of contrasting the NDP to the Grits in the 1990 election. Public auto insurance and the continued ban on Sunday shopping were seen as chimerical. When push came to shove, the NDP couldn't implement public auto insurance and didn't live up to its promise to maintain the law against Sunday shopping, much to the chagrin of Kormos and party stalwarts such as Mel Swart.

The party that had made so much hay out of environmental issues ended up doing very little that was positive in the five years it was in power. Bob Rae, who had once been a Temagami tree-hugger, didn't even bring in recycling quotas. Instead, he banned incineration and rail-hauling garbage to Kirkland Lake, leaving Metro to cope with its own garbage crisis.

The social contract, said Kormos, was "disastrous." It was badly researched and developed on the run. The legislation is not clear, and there is still confusion over what happens when the deal expires in 1996.

To compound all his failures to deliver his promises, Rae became ever more reclusive. He withdrew from any direct contact with the public and even limited his access to members of his caucus. He acquired a "Tuxedo fetish," preferring to wine and dine with the elites of society. Kormos complained that Rae was more at home at a cocktail party with diplomats and high rollers than he was in a union hall or at the plant gate. As well, some ministers didn't understand the public relations function that went along with the job. Kormos wanted ministers to go into ridings and take the heat for various NDP policies and to take some time to praise the work of the local MPP. He remembered some riding speeches in which a minister didn't even mention the local member.

And, he added, the party was curiously not very political. Many of the appointments made by Rae didn't go to party faithful.

"We had long-time NDP supporters who couldn't get appointments to the most innocuous little things because there was this obsession with being sanitary and not willing to be accused of patronage and not being willing to fight the issue."

There is nothing wrong with patronage, Kormos said, as long as the appointee is competent. He wanted a woman, or someone who fit the government's equity targets, appointed head of the Liquor Control Board when that position came vacant. However, Rae chose long-time Tory Andy Brandt. He reappointed Frank Drea, another long-time Tory, head of the Ontario Racing Commission, although he was later dumped.

There was very little "democracy" within the party, Kormos said. Ministers often didn't consult with backbenchers on issues affecting their ridings. Caucus members were rarely called to the premier's office to discuss what was going on in their part of the province. To compound matters, the New Democrats had an "adolescent" attitude towards the "bourgeois, capitalist press that's out to get us." They had a pathological hatred of the *Toronto Sun*. While Bob Rae's diplomat buddies read the *Globe* with their Perrier at lunch, the premier hadn't figured out that the people who actually voted for him and his New Democrats were working stiffs who found the tabloid just the right size for their lunchpails.

"Whether you think the *Sun* is great news reportage or not, it doesn't change the reality that that's what most blue-collar people in southern Ontario tend to be reading." Kormos said that his caucus colleagues would frown and cluck any time he talked to the *Sun*, and when he appeared as a SUNshine Boy, it drove some of them over the top.

Kormos recalled one incident which summed up for him Rae's disregard for his caucus colleagues and his political aides. It happened shortly after the John Piper affair, when a senior aide to Rae was caught trying to release privileged information to a *Sun* reporter. A television interviewer asked Rae a question about the people he relied on for advice. Rae answered that first he relied on his wife. Secondly, his brother. And thirdly, David Peterson and John Turner.

"There was no mention of his cabinet, his caucus, his brain trust, the inner circle," Kormos recalled. It was a curious response.

Kormos said that while you have to admire the premier for his honesty, it would have been wise to have tempered that honesty with a little common sense. At the very least he should have made some passing reference to his party and pretended to be a team player. He should have told the reporter that he consulted his cabinet and caucus.

But the good side of Bob Rae is that he is nothing if not honest. Frankly honest, brutally honest. A person who hates confrontation. "He'll not want to hear something if it's going to put him in a position where he'll feel compelled to compromise his integrity," Kormos said. He tends to be a "hear no evil see no evil" type of person.

Rae is an extremely private person. He is not close to caucus members. In his five years in office, Kormos estimated that he spoke to Rae no more than three times. But Kormos admired the former premier's commitment to his family. Rae made it clear that his mornings didn't start early because he wanted to be home for breakfast with his three daughters. Others commented on Rae's strong sense of morality. He is enormously generous in giving to charity, but he keeps quiet about it. According to one former colleague, when Rae was in opposition, he was presented with a plaque for donating the most to charity of anyone in the legislature. Rae was extremely embarrassed by the award.

What sunk Rae, Kormos said, was his desire to have a hand in every decision. The premier tended to be very much a one-man show. "I think he had a very strong sense of his own brilliance," Kormos said of Rae.

Coming into the election, however, Rae became deceived by the polls. They showed that he was more popular than his own party. There was support out there for the social contract. Unfortunately, it was not among people who would ever vote NDP.

"It was Tory types who agreed with the social contract. That doesn't mean they were going to vote for New Democrats. Just because people thought Bob was a better leader than the others, a better speaker and perhaps more integrous, didn't mean they were going to vote for us. They still didn't like either his ideology, or his failure to keep commitments. So the campaign strategy very soon began to focus on Bob Rae as the leader. It was going to be a leadership campaign – I'm part of the Bob Rae team."

And that, said Kormos, was where things really derailed. In Kormos's riding of Welland-Thorold, Rae was wildly unpopular with the union types. While polls showed Rae and Harris neck-and-neck in popularity, the NDP leader was not popular at all in the blue-collar, working-class areas where the party traditionally drew its strength. "Bob Rae wasn't going to carry people. He was a little bit of an albatross," Kormos remarked. Kormos's personal standing in the riding, and the fact that he had stood up to Rae, won him re-election.

Rae's caucus resembled a fraternity or sorority, he said. Everyone wanted to belong. No one wanted to speak out and risk having done to them what had happened to Kormos. People were so fearful of being sent to Coventry by the inner circle that they didn't speak out. Kormos's run-in with party brass, however, helped re-elect him. He'd knock on doors, and people would tell him that they didn't like Bob Rae.

"Listen, I ain't crazy about him either," Kormos would reply.

But his was an attitude few in the party shared. Or, at least, few in the party cared to admit to.

Bob Rae took things personally. Kormos would crack jokes in speeches about Rae's popularity, and the former premier didn't have enough sense to laugh at himself.

"Bob was never comfortable with that shirt-sleeves approach to politics. He really should be a diplomat," said Kormos. "He was very private, very isolated, didn't trust plain folk for their political insight. It was the exception to have ministers who were political and politically skilful." Rae is politically "pristine." He didn't want to be seen hurting or criticizing politically correct groups.

One of the arguments that swayed Rae in the auto insurance debacle was the prediction that 11,000 women would lose their jobs. Rae always liked to be seen supporting women's issues, and Kormos said that this was partly his rationale for scrapping the plan. When the Patti Starr scandal broke, Rae was hesitant to criticize her because she was (a) a woman and (b) Jewish. Kormos claimed that Rae didn't want to be perceived as anti-woman or anti-Semitic.

And Rae was meticulous about obscene or coarse language. He really didn't like vulgarity. The only time Kormos heard Rae use an expletive was when the Liberal government dropped an issue on the order paper late at night, and Rae told the government House leader what to do. Rae later apologized to his caucus, which prompted Kormos to suggest that the premier go on the record with his comments. They probably would have increased the party's popularity in Kormos's blue-collar riding.

Rae hates confrontation. Once you cross him, you're off his dance card for good. Former cabinet minister Zanana Akande ran afoul of Rae on policy development. She was committed to the agenda espoused in the 1990 election. When the government strayed from that agenda, she quit, thoroughly disillusioned.

At one point, Kormos said, he was so worried about the polls, so concerned about the way the party had alienated all their traditional supporters, that he feared that the NDP might lose their official party status. He knew that they had walked roughshod over both the Liberals and the Tories, and he was worried that neither party would be prepared to extend any favors to what was left of the NDP if they were decimated. Kormos was pleasantly surprised that the New Democrats elected seventeen members.

Kormos was left absolutely speechless by those party members who even late in the campaign refused to accept the fact that they weren't going to be returned as the government. He was urging the party to change gears, to start running a campaign to become the official Opposition. It was an attractive strategy. With the Tories surging in the polls, Kormos urged his colleagues to go head-to-head with Harris and present the NDP as the only party who could take on the Tory cuts.

"We couldn't shift gears," Kormos said. There were some members of the NDP caucus who were mesmerized by their five years in government. They felt that one term in office automatically deserved a second. Even after the election, there are some within the diminished NDP caucus who feel they must conduct themselves in a dignified fashion as they await their inevitable return to power.

The famous fiery rhetoric of the NDP has fizzled out. However, continued Kormos, it will be difficult for the Liberals to oppose the Tory cuts. The voting public figured that the Liberal platform was identical to the Tory platform. How can the Liberals attack the Tories in the legislature? He said that the NDP will be the only effective opposition to the government.

"I'll be waving the Red Book right next to the Blue Book," he said.

New Democrat strategists should have seen the writing on the wall. The famed grass-roots New Democratic machinery just wasn't there. This was partly a result of the 1993 federal campaign when the New Democrats were nearly wiped off the electoral map. A lot of ridings couldn't get workers out.

"Campaign workers were just so tired of having doors slammed in their faces. That was always our forte, but canvassers in all ridings were hard to get. The unions weren't sending people out to do that basic door-knocking, foot work, the hard work. We didn't have good propaganda from the central headquarters. And Bob Rae simply didn't cut it. And we weren't capable of shifting gears."

Many New Democrats still don't understand what happened. Kormos contends that it is adolescent to believe that there was some kind of conspiracy among a capitalist and racist electorate to defeat the NDP. That was paranoia. The New Democrats were out of touch with the people.

Moreover, many of those elected in the 1990 sweep were one-issue candidates. Some became New Democrats only a few days before the writ for the election was dropped. Many of them espoused yuppie concerns for trendy issues at the direct expense of the more traditional union point of view. Insiders started to see warning signals. Increasingly, the leader retreated ever more into himself, insisting that everything had to come across his desk. Cabinet ministers lost contact with the people. And there was a feeling within the party that the government should be all things to all people. At one time, there was an obvious concerted effort to portray Bob Rae as a friend of Bay Street. It was a completely wasted effort, as far as Kormos is concerned.

"If I were the president of a bank, I wouldn't vote for the NDP," he said. "The theme became, we are the government of all the people, and we tried to be that. And in the process, we lost everybody."

Other observers paint a similar picture. One veteran Queen's Park pundit remarked that it was almost as if Rae dropped the election writ without being ready to fight the election. He compared the lack of NDP preparedness to the Allies planning the D-Day landing without having any troops or landing craft to carry off the mission. The NDP were woefully behind in preparations for the election. Rae tried to make light of his party fortunes at a press conference on the day of the election call, by parodying a line from Forrest Gump that "elections are like a box of chocolates." But he should have realized that there were precious few chocolates in his box and that the ones he did have were hard in the centre. At the beginning of the campaign, it was tough for the media to find out who was in charge. Early press releases didn't even have campaign phone numbers on them.

The issues weren't on their side. The Tories made great hay over welfare. Tony Silipo, the social services minister, only reluctantly admitted to the existence of welfare fraud. His program to eliminate it was too little, too late. Had he tried it two years earlier, and had there been any visible improvement, the voters might have bought their program. At least it would have made it a lot tougher for Harris to have used the "welfare card" to his advantage.

Even with the polls showing NDP support sticking at 17 percent, or at the most 20 percent, there were still some ministers who talked about "second-term initiatives." They really believed that the electorate was going to give them another chance.

Meanwhile, business had ground to a halt at Queen's Park. The legislature sat briefly during November and December 1994, and it was not recalled before the election. The entire spring of 1995 was lost time. There was no budget, only a pre-election financial statement aimed more at making the NDP look good rather than setting out any reasoned and rational financial program.

The NDP failed to push through the kind of labor legislation its pro-union supporters would have liked. While the right complained about Bill 40's pro-labor bias, NDP supporters within the labor movement saw it as a watered-down piece of legislation and a cop-out. And there were some party members who thought that if the government was going to take the flak for the weaker legislation anyway, they might as well have toughened it up and given the unions what they wanted. Tougher legislation would have produced more blue-collar votes for the NDP. Again, it was a case of too little, too late.

In a curious way, the Bob Rae campaign of 1995 started to look like the Mike Harris campaign of 1990. We can't promise you anything, Rae said, the message being that he was the only honest politician. It didn't catch on. The NDP's massive, pre-election promises of untold millions for projects around the province was a cynical vote-buying spree.

Veteran Queen's Park observer Graham Murray said that Rae's

image as an academic, a Rhodes scholar, and a member of the elite didn't help him very much. There was a feeling that Rae was a snob who didn't understand the common man.

"Perhaps being very bright is debilitating in politics," Murray said.

Chapter Twenty-four

Free Spirits

L et's hope that Prime Minister Jean Chrétien and the federal Liberals were paying attention to the Ontario election. There is a lesson here, you see, for those who buck the tide and vote against their own caucus, especially politicians from small towns and rural constituencies, and that lesson is this: voters will love you for your honesty and return you to power, no matter what the rest of the country or province does.

Take, for example, Peter Kormos, the small-town NDP maverick who bucked Premier Bob Rae and the NDP establishment on public auto insurance and Sunday shopping. He was returned handily to Queen's Park, but all around him his New Democrat colleagues dropped like flies.

During the campaign he asked people one basic question: "What kind of an MPP do you want? Do you want a voice, or just an echo?"

The answer came back loud and clear.

"People voted for a representative who seemed independent, and who didn't simply follow the caucus line. The public was very conscious of the fact that I had not reneged or contradicted what I had said on Sunday shopping or public auto insurance," Kormos said in an interview shortly after the election. He sensed a frustration among voters with the punishment which Chrétien meted out to caucus members who didn't toe the party line.

"People are pretty disappointed in Chrétien's response. When you've got a majority of that size, you're not going to defeat legislation by letting a number of members vote against it."

Over in Elgin County, Peter North said that Chrétien's unceremonious attempt to dump Warren Allmand from a committee shortly before provincial election day – for voting against the federal budget – helped re-elect North as an independent. North quit the NDP caucus over an alleged incident involving a young woman, a job, and no sex. Rae called in the cops to investigate, and no evidence of wrongdoing was found. Obviously, North's constituents have faith in him, since they sent him back to Queen's Park as their MPP, the first independent to be elected to the Ontario parliament in over sixty years. The last time a candidate with no party affiliation was elected was in 1934, when Morrison MacBride won in Brantford.

"Some of the decisions Chrétien made played into our hands," North said in a recent interview. "People are ticked off. They're upset. They've had enough. They don't want to see sixty-five or seventy people all lining up in a row to jump off a cliff like lemmings."

Curiously, both North and Kormos ran into enormous opposition to the new federal gun-control legislation in their rural ridings. Neither supports the new Grit gun law. North wanted tougher penalties for gun-related crimes, while Kormos said it's a "wacky bit of legislation."

North claimed that his constituents were happy to send a renegade back to Queen's Park. In fact, he said, support for him increased the more his opponents raised the fact that he would be a "lone voice in the wilderness."

For both Kormos and North, constituency work is the prime reason for their success. They have done it well. In small towns and cities with stable voting populations, it counts for practically everything. Chrétien should remember that the next time he's tempted to strong-arm rebel caucus members.

Chapter Twenty-five

You Say You Want a Revolution?

A ll told, it was a risky revolution. Publishing the Common Sense Revolution a year before the election was a bold move. This is not how elections are run in Ontario, where policy statements are dished out day-by-day and fed carefully to the media during a thirty-seven-day run-up to the vote. Hand-picking young people, none of whom had held the reins of power before, to run your campaign was another brilliant stroke. All of them had countless hours of campaign experience, but they'd always been on the periphery. They had no experience in running an election campaign from top to bottom, from beginning to end. And they came from warring factions within the party. For a long time, party insiders had kept them out of the hallowed circle of power. Some of the movers and shakers weren't at all happy to have this young, brash group running their campaign. They were too aggressive, too right wing. Some in the old guard were reluctant to relinquish the reins to the youngsters – until the last ten days of the campaign.

As soon as the Tories started to rise in the opinion polls, so too did their fortunes. Money started flowing in, and workers were easier to find. At last, new blood was coursing through the once-hardened arteries of the Big Blue Machine.

For the campaign team, there were several lessons in all this. Never again would the party be allowed to build up the kind of deficits which they inherited. The accumulated debt crippled them, and it took many years to replenish it.

Tom Long and Leslie Noble made a commitment to one another and to Mike Harris at the beginning of the campaign that they would groom the next generation of campaign managers. To each position at campaign headquarters, Long and Noble attached a designate from the youth organization, who learned the different elements of managing a political campaign. The Tories put young people in very responsible, decision-making roles. Jeff Nathan, Leslie Noble's assistant, and many other young people were free to attend any meeting. They were never shut out. All this was a conscious, deliberate effort to avoid another ten-year vacuum in leadership. This young Tory team believed absolutely in their leader and his message. They had complete faith that once the electorate heard the message, they too would believe it.

In the last ten days of the campaign, critics of the Tories accused them of pushing "hot buttons," of appealing to the meanness of the electorate. But, countered Leslie Noble, the hot buttons were only hot buttons once the Tories started winning the election.

"Call them hot buttons, I guess," said Noble. "You can also call them issues that people have an enormous amount of frustration over because government (a) won't talk about them and (b) won't do anything about them. And as long as you are afraid to talk about problems, as long as you want to play politics with them, then nobody is ever going to solve the problem, it's only going to get worse."

Problems such as poverty and equality of opportunity will never be solved as long as critics and commentators and special interest groups keep accusing the people who raise those issues of being racist or anti-poor.

"That is really the root cause of people's frustrations," said Noble. "I don't believe that there are very many Canadians or Ontarians who genuinely want to see any single mom starving in the street. There's nobody, or very few, who want to see someone discriminated against because of the color of their skin, or their religion. But what they don't want is to have solutions that cause as much harm to other sectors as the initial problem did. So, for once, someone was willing to talk about the problems.

"It wasn't until we started moving in the polls that the Liberals and NDP started calling them hot buttons," she said.

Caucus members told the campaign organization that there was an incredible level of frustration in their constituencies over welfare and employment equity. It wasn't that people wanted to grind others down. They acknowledged that racism and discrimination in the workplace were real problems, but they felt that the government was only making those problems worse with their legislation.

Oddly, both the NDP and the Liberals recognized to some degree this same frustration. The NDP started to move on welfare fraud, for example, although their efforts amounted to very little. And the Liberals tried to articulate policies on welfare and employment equity but ended up confusing and angering the voters with bafflegab such as "mandatory opportunity."

"It wasn't until we started winning the election that those became hot buttons that were bad things. As long as they were serving the NDP, they were things that needed to be done. As long as they were serving the Liberals, they were things that needed to be done. The minute they started driving numbers for us, and people started to believe our policies, they became hot buttons and they became bad things and people started accusing us of being brown shirts," Noble pointed out.

The Tories had such immense confidence in their platform and their leader that they told their people at candidate training school that everything would happen in the last ten days of the campaign. It wouldn't be until that time, when people actually started paying attention to the election, that things would move. They were convinced that once people took a look at Mike Harris and read the CSR, they would vote for him.

"Mike had a high level of confidence in the policies and there was good reason for that – it came directly from the people all across the province. It's not like we sat down and wrote something and then said, 'Oooh, we hope this is going to work.'

"We said, 'We know this is going to work because this is what we have been building toward with the help of everyone in this province.'"

Tory focus groups after the debate showed that Harris had scored highest when he talked about credibility and honesty and that McLeod scored lowest when she talked about the same ideas and same-sex benefits.

"The conclusion was that she had burned a group of people. Whether you believe, or don't believe, that same-sex benefits is something that should or shouldn't be done.

"The impression these people had in these focus groups is that she had, for political gain, used a group and then turned around and burned them. And if she was doing that to them, how could they believe anything she said on anything else?" Noble asked.

There is a great irony in all of this. Media pundits and many Liberals believed that the flap over same-sex benefits was in large part responsible for the Liberal defeat in Victoria-Haliburton. The Tories disagreed. They said that their videos aimed at undecided voters won the riding for them. It was widely perceived by the electorate that Lyn McLeod flip-flopped on same-sex benefits. It was a flip-flop triggered in part by the Liberals' inability to win the Victoria-Haliburton by-election. So, ironically, while the flip-flop over same-sex benefits didn't cause the Liberal loss in the by-election, it may have contributed to their defeat in the general election.

"There didn't seemed to be a core set of beliefs. There didn't seem to be a set of guiding principles. It seemed that they believed in winning at whatever cost and the public is smart enough to figure that out."

After the election, a flurry of left-wing commentators blamed Harris's win on the "meanness" of the electorate, without explaining why an electorate that was supposedly smart enough five years earlier to elect the NDP could turn on their masters. Happily, the Queen's Park media refused to be stampeded into this group-think mentality.

"I think the difference this time and with this gallery is that there are a lot of independent thinkers there," explained Noble. "Sometimes you go through a bit of a pack mentality. But there are a lot of independent thinkers there who aren't willing to take the party line, the paper line. I think it's a very healthy dynamic there."

In the last week of the campaign, the Harris tour went on a

long northern trip. Gossip had the Tory campaign team keeping Harris away from the Metro media. That simply wasn't the case, said Noble, since a busload of reporters followed Harris all over Ontario, and the campaign spent 65 percent of its time in Metro, which has the greatest concentration of seats.

The final swing through the north was an attempt to capture additional seats there. Noble regretted that the tour didn't spend more time in northern Ontario. Voters in the north don't make up their minds until the last minute, and they tend to look at what's happening in the rest of the province before joining a bandwagon.

"In retrospect, I think we probably should have gone in a week earlier and we might have been able to generate some momentum, which we never did generate in the north. It was just starting."

Noble believed that the Tories could have won Rainy River (where they came second, trailing NDP incumbent Howard Hampton by only a handful of votes), as well as Cochrane South and Algoma-Manitoulin. While the two most powerful men in the Harris administration – the premier himself and his lieutenant Ernie Eves – represent northern ridings, the Tories hold only those two seats in all of the north.

There were few disappointments for the Tories. After all, they did win 82 seats. However, their two Ottawa candidates – Greg Joy and Linda Thom – didn't make the cut. And in Kingston, *Toronto Sun* columnist Sally Barnes, a press secretary to former premier Bill Davis, lost a heartbreaker to former mayor John Gerretson.

There were some oddities about the 1995 election – things that might have been and very nearly were. About ten days before voting day, Mike Harris's principal secretary, David Lindsay, who was at Harris's side in the leader's bus throughout the campaign, got a call from a senior New Democrat campaign worker.

"Are your numbers showing what our numbers are showing?" asked the New Democrat.

"I don't know," said Lindsay, "What are you showing?" New Democrat figures had the Tories at almost 50 percent. But, more importantly, they also showed the Liberals and New Democrats neck-and-neck for second place, with the New Democrats starting to pull ahead of the Liberals. Also, the concentration of the vote was such that there was a real chance that Bob Rae would become leader of Her Majesty's Loyal Opposition.

The Tories indeed had figures showing the Grits dropping. The concentration or diffusion of votes can determine the distribution of seats in the legislature. In the 1993 federal election, for example, Preston Manning had 1.6 votes in limited areas and Kim Campbell had 1.6 million votes spread across Canada. Reform returned to Parliament with 53 seats, while the PCs returned with two.

Some pundits still believe that had the election campaign lasted another week, the NDP could have formed the official Opposition. Voters saw only two options – on the left was Bob Rae and on the right was Mike Harris. The Liberals had collapsed down the middle. It was a scenario which Mike Harris had predicted in a caucus meeting more than a year before the election. "This campaign is going to come down to Bob Rae and Mike Harris," the Tory leader told his colleagues.

If only he'd let Bob Rae and Lyn McLeod in on the secret.

Chapter Twenty-six

The Writ Drops

F riday, 28 April, dawned chilly and blustery in Ontario. Despite the dismal weather, there was a buzz of excitement around Queen's Park. Today's the day, reporters predicted, when Premier Bob Rae was sure to walk the walk, from his office at the south-east corner of the second floor of the legislative building to Lieutenant-Governor Hal Jackman's apartment at the north-west corner, to drop the writ on Jackman's desk. Sure enough, in the middle of the afternoon Rae emerged from his office with his wife, Arlene Perly, at his side and strode purposefully towards Jackman's office, writ in hand.

So the 35th Session of the Ontario legislature died. Not with a bang, although a bomb threat earlier promised more fireworks than anyone had bargained for. Not even with a whimper, since the premier came out swinging with a Forrest Gump-like aphorism.

"Every election is like a box of chocolates," he told media at a press conference shortly after he visited Jackman. "You never know what you'll find inside." The date he picked for the election was 8 June, giving voters forty days, instead of the customary thirty-seven, to check out the candidates. You couldn't help thinking back to the day his crew arrived at Queen's Park four and a half years earlier, with hope in their hearts and hayseeds in their hair. A fistful of scandals and one social contract later, his government was poised to nosedive into oblivion.

By 28 April, the Tories were tired. They had done all their work. Mike Harris's speeches were all written; their game plan was in place. Everything had been hashed and rehashed so many times that they were starting to chase their own tails, to second-guess their carefully laid plans. But once the election was called, they were the first party out of the gate.

The epicentre of the Tory campaign was the ninth-floor boardroom at their University Avenue headquarters. Only the key campaign workers were allowed into this private world created by Leslie Noble. Campaign workers spent a weekend painting the walls revolutionary blue. The place boasted a putting machine, exercise bikes, and video games to help relieve the day-to-day tension of the campaign. A "bat phone," a spider-like contraption that sat in the middle of their conference table, directly connected them to the leader's bus. It was an unwritten rule of the campaign that this phone had to be answered by the second ring. The boardroom was a very private place, reflecting the characters of the young people that led the campaign to victory.

Days started early with a 7 a.m. briefing around the table. The whole team would be there – Tom Long, Leslie Noble, Alister Campbell, Scott Munnoch, Mitch Patten, Peter Varley, and Dave the dog. Paul Rhodes, the senior media advisor, would give the team a run-down on what had appeared in the print and electronic media that morning. He and Varley would tell them what to expect from various outlets. Tom Long watched the noon and six o'clock newscasts, taping and replaying clips of Mike Harris's performance and the odd campaign slip-up. As the campaign progressed, it was clear that Harris was looking better and better.

Another strictly enforced rule of the campaign was that once a decision had been taken, everyone abided by it. If a mistake was made, there was no finger-pointing, no recriminations. The disgrace would be shared equally. It was understood that they would swim or sink as a team. And no individual person, except perhaps Mike Harris, would take credit for a victory.

The Tory campaign was quick to react to bad stories. When a protester bopped Mike Harris's OPP bodyguard over the head in a demonstration on the Danforth in Toronto, not everyone in the media had caught the action. The campaign team quickly made a tape of the six o'clock news that clearly showed the action and sent it to the bus. On another occasion, an Ottawa-area Liberal MPP called the Tories "brownshirts." The Tories called *Sun* reporter James Wallace on his cell phone and quoted the Ottawa newspaper item to him. He was in a scrum with Lyn McLeod at the time and questioned her on the item, catching the Liberal leader off guard.

Above all, it was a fun time for the Tories. There was a tremendous amount of camaraderie. While it's always easier to keep spirits up when you're winning, it wasn't the party's soaring popularity in the polls that kept the campaign team together as a cohesive unit. Things started to turn around only during the last couple of weeks. They'd stuck together through the lean times when the polls were unfriendly.

Much of the teamwork's success was attributed to Leslie Noble, who had built the team, smoothed ruffled feathers, and kept the group ticking. But Tom Long also deserved credit. He gave the team a focus and dealt with the criticism, some from within the party. Their political opponents dismissed the Tories as wacky "Ayn Rand freaks." But Long kept his cool.

He did it because he believed in Mike Harris and the message. The work which he put into the campaign was certainly a labor of beliefs, of values. He was not a hired gun, brought in to use clever strategies to bring Harris to power. Long said that he will only work on another campaign if someone he believes in comes along. Now that the election is over he has returned to his job in the private sector. He's a partner in Egon Zehnder International, a firm of management consultants. He took a long leave of absence to work on the campaign.

Long, Noble, and other campaign workers suffered through the daily opprobrium of the *Toronto Star*, which refused to believe that the Tories were about to pull off an election victory. The Tories declined to meet with the editorial board at the *Star* because they knew that the paper would never endorse them. Any formal meeting with the *Star* would have wasted precious campaign time. Long told the team time and again, "We are going to go through the wall of fire, and we're going to go through it together. And when we come through, we will have won or lost."

Make no mistake, the Tory victory was not some forty-day miracle. Mike Harris and his team worked for five years to reverse the political humiliation which the party had suffered in 1985. They succeeded in bringing the party back to power. Harris will make a great premier, said insiders, because he understands what he is doing and why. And he will do what he said he would do, unlike his predecessor in the premier's office.

In the final analysis, said Paul Rhodes, the Liberals made two basic strategy errors. One, they left the Tories alone for the first two weeks, allowing them to get all kinds of air time, which helped them drive up their numbers. While the Tories had a plan if their numbers went up, it seemed to them that the Liberals didn't have a plan if *their* numbers dropped. And they knew they had to slip.

Two, the Red Book was such a disaster that by the end of the campaign, the Liberals had abandoned it altogether.

"I can remember sitting in the media monitoring room up at headquarters watching the 6 o'clock news," Rhodes recalled. "And somebody said, 'When did we last see the Red Book, how long has it been?' and it suddenly dawned on me that they had abandoned their entire campaign platform to go into an attack mode.

"So when people turned on their TVs in the last week or ten days of the campaign when they are making decisions, they saw Mike Harris with a plan and Bob Rae and Lyn McLeod attacking Mike Harris. So the only message getting out was ours and the people had no idea where the others stood. I think it was a critical error," said Rhodes, a veteran of many campaigns, including the catastrophic Larry Grossman one in 1987.

But the Red Book wasn't the only Grit mistake. They committed their first and perhaps biggest error when they misread the entrails from the Victoria-Haliburton by-election. Tory data showed that their videos carried the day. Most pundits mistakenly attributed the Liberal defeat to "homophobia" in rural Ontario, a view that may have forced Grit strategists to back away from support for same-sex legislation.

Another problem was the inability of the old guard within the Liberal Party to let go of the reins of power. It had been a tough thing for the Tories to do, but they had done it. Young Tories suddenly found themselves working without a net, so to speak. While they all had worked on campaigns before, they'd never been in charge. But they were lucky. The Hugh Segals and John Torys stayed to one side, although when called on for help and advice, they gave more than they'd been asked for. Segal for one did many on-camera media interviews and was briefed regularly by the campaign team. Paul Rhodes said that without extensive coaching from John Tory, he could never have negotiated the tricky debate deal. The old Tories let the young Tories step into their shoes and walk away with a stunning election victory.

Whatever the pundits say, there was no magic formula. This election wasn't won by clever tricks and an ability to manipulate headlines or by hot buttons and a meanness of spirit. It was vision, five years of hard work, a plan, and a set of core beliefs that appealed to the voters.

Chapter Twenty-seven

Red Book versus Revolution

I t was a campaign of Red Book versus Revolution, spouses and houses, debates and tax rebates, and endless hours spent getting the message out in hundreds of communities from Kapuskasing to Cornwall to Windsor.

If armies march on their stomachs, political armies these days march on their cell phones, fax machines, state-of-the-art computers, and the high-priced satellite trucks that can beam the news live from just about anywhere in Ontario. This was a high-tech campaign. The Tory bus was a travelling electronic temple, with little cell phone antennas sticking up like minarets from the roof.

Of course, stomachs are important too. It was a campaign in which the entire entourage – political leaders as well as the army of media types following them – marched on bacon on a bun, toasted bagels, and endless rounds of pizza. Food on the Tory bus was lavish, and the fridge was well-stocked with liquid refreshment. For one reporter on the Harris bus, partying was so easy that he almost got whisked away to Windsor with the Tories. He was supposed to be covering the Liberals who were heading for Kitchener.

One of the delights of the campaign was the utter professionalism of the party staff on each of the buses. No matter what the polls showed, no matter how critical the media had been that day, party workers on each bus maintained, at least on the surface, a stoic, cheerful facade. Well, okay, the Liberal bus may have left the occasional *Toronto Sun* columnist standing in a cloud of bus exhaust at the curb. By and large, though, they were pretty nice.

What was perhaps most encouraging was the Tory campaign itself. They dealt in positives. They wanted to give people something to vote for rather than someone to vote against. There were no dirty tricks in their campaign. The Grits may have complained at the end about the weathervane ad depicting Lyn McLeod twisting in the wind, but it was hardly a shocker.

Some Grits, meanwhile, got bogged down trying out "real time" campaigning. The contest in High Park-Swansea, in which Tory Derwyn Shea nudged out Elaine Ziemba, was one of the dirtiest in town. Grit Ted Lojko first tried a "push poll" – a U.S. style smear tactic – to discredit Shea. Then, at the end of the campaign, he distributed more negative literature throughout the riding. None of it had any effect, and Lojko ended up a poor third.

Negative tactics backfired on Grit Dianne Poole in Eglinton. She came out with a nasty picture of Mike Harris and the incredible statement that he wanted to throw renters out on the street. Then, in a last-ditch attempt to grab support, she tried to distance herself from McLeod. It didn't work. She was trounced by Tory Bill Saunderson.

The failure to get *Sun* columnist Sally Barnes elected in Kingston and the Islands was one of the few disappointments experienced by the Tories on election night. Barnes, a former press secretary to Bill Davis, was up against tough opposition in the person of former Kingston mayor John Gerretsen. Barnes knew her way around Queen's Park and was common sense personified. She had an excellent grasp of provincial politics, and she would have been a feisty addition to the Harris cabinet. Oh, well. Kingston's loss is the *Toronto Sun's* gain. At least we can look forward to her wonderfully witty columns again.

Two other *Sun* people ran in the election. The paper's home delivery supervisor, Dan Newman, topped the polls in Scarborough Centre, and its former day-one business manager Jim Brown, defeated New Democrat Anne Swarbrick in Scarborough West. Brown epitomizes everything Harris was talking about during the campaign. He's the quintessential small entrepreneur who's established himself with a combination of hard work and business savvy.

Curiously, the only independent MPP is former New

Democrat Peter North, who was re-elected in Elgin, despite being dropped from the caucus for allegedly offering a job to a young woman in return for sexual favors. A police investigation found no wrongdoing. His dalliance occurred in a pub called the Loose Moose. But voters forgave North for his misdemeanor and returned him to Queen's Park. New Democrat Hugh MacGinnis ran a distant fourth in the riding, behind Jim Williams for the Tories and Barry Fitzgerald for the Grits.

Another surprise upset occurred in Beaches-Woodbine. No, New Democrat cabinet minister Frances Lankin wasn't defeated. The riding has been an NDP fortress from the time when Marion Bryden represented it. The surprise was the poor showing of Steven Lautens. Son of the late *Star* columnist Gary Lautens, he had toiled endlessly in the riding and was supposedly giving a Lankin a run for her money. Instead, Tory Lynda Buffett, who threw her hat in the ring only at the last minute, came second.

The Tories' dedication to Mike Harris and the party's single-minded focus on the concerns of the people ultimately won the day. Campaign co-chairs Tom Long and Leslie Noble were young in age but seasoned campaigners at the provincial and federal levels. The Tories took a huge gamble when they came out with their Common Sense Revolution in 1994. It was a take-it or leave-it, right-wing agenda that had the Grits and the NDP rolling their eyes and hurling around "Chainsaw Mike" epithets. But at a time of massive voter cynicism and a general lack of trust in any party, voters opted for their plan over McLeod's promise of everything – and nothing. At the close of the day, voters rejected the mushy middle with a vengeance.

As the campaign progressed, it became evident that politicians aboard the Liberal bus were getting a tad frustrated with my columns. The first hint, and it wasn't very subtle, came on the day they drove off without me. That's why reporters were shocked when the Grits pulled into a Dairy Queen during the last week of the tour.

So what did I order? Yes, you guessed. A Blizzard.

Now, doesn't that send chills right through you?

INDEX